10664734

Past Masters

AQUINAS Anthony Kenny
DANTE George Holmes
HUME A. J. Ayer
JESUS Humphrey Carpenter
MARX Peter Singer
PASCAL Alban Krailsheimer

Forthcoming
AUGUSTINE Henry Chadwick
BACH Denis Arnold
BACON Anthony Quinton
BAYLE Elisabeth Labrousse
BERKELEY J. Urmson
BURKE C. B. Macpherson
CARLYLE A. L. Le Quesne
CONFUCIUS Raymond Dawson
COPERNICUS Owen Gingerich
DARWIN Jonathan Howard
DIDEROT Peter France
ENGELS Terrell Carver
ERASMUS James McConica
GALILEO Stillman Drake
GODWIN Alan Ryan
GOETHE J. P. Stern
HERZEN Aileen Kelly
HOMER Jasper Griffin
MACHIAVELLI Quentin Skinner
MILL William Thomas
MONTAIGNE Peter Burke
MORRIS Peter Stansky
NEWTON P. M. Rattansi
ROUSSEAU John McManners
ST PAUL Tom Mills
SHAKESPEARE Germaine Greer
TOLSTOY C. H. Gifford
and others

Alban Krailsheimer

PASCAL

Oxford   Toronto   Melbourne

OXFORD UNIVERSITY PRESS

1980

Oxford University Press, Walton Street, Oxford OX2 6DP

OXFORD LONDON GLASGOW
NEW YORK TORONTO MELBOURNE WELLINGTON
KUALA LUMPUR SINGAPORE JAKARTA HONG KONG TOKYO
DELHI BOMBAY CALCUTTA MADRAS KARACHI
NAIROBI DAR ES SALAAM CAPE TOWN

British Library Cataloguing in Publication Data

Krailsheimer, Alban John
  Pascal. – (Past Masters).
  1. Pascal, Blaise
  I. Series
  194   B1903   79-41292

  ISBN 0-19-287513-2
  ISBN 0-19-287512-4   Pbk

*Set, printed and bound in Great Britain by
Cox & Wyman Ltd, Reading*

Contents

Note: All references to the *Pensées* are to the arrangement observed in the various editions of Louis Lafuma, translated by myself in Penguin Classics. The numbering in all other editions and translations is quite different, though some editions include a concordance.

The two following abbreviations are used in the text:

Apology	*Apology for the Christian Religion*
PLs	*Provincial Letters*

1 Life

More than three hundred years after Pascal's death, many thousands of people each year buy the *Pensées* without knowing anything about the author or his life. They are clearly influenced by the book as though it were anonymous. Because it was left unfinished, much of it remains in fragmentary form, and this is often felt to be an attraction, which offers memorable aphorisms untrammelled by any context. The incurable narcissism of human beings makes the *Pensées* an irresistible mirror in which to regard their own thoughts and feelings rather than a window revealing the man who wrote them.

Pascal said that what we find in Montaigne is in us rather than in Montaigne (*Pensées* 689); the same is manifestly true of him. It is true, too, that the unfinished state of the *Pensées*, undeniably Pascal's masterpiece, may suggest an unfinished genius, a life cut short before fulfilment, and as such hardly worthy of serious attention. It is as though Mozart's life could be dismissed as incomplete because he left the Requiem and other masterpieces unfinished. In fact the *Pensées* are the record and culmination of a life full of remarkable achievement. Pascal, who died at thirty-nine, like Mozart, who died at thirty-four, must not be measured on a simple actuarial scale, nor must the *Pensées* be read as an anthology of sublime, virtually anonymous graffiti, a kind of Wayside Pulpit. Precisely because the work is unfinished, it is to the man and his life we must turn for elucidation of so much that remains obscure in the text. Perhaps the man and his life may even enable us to find a truer reflection of ourselves in the mirror of the *Pensées*.

Pascal knew only too well that his contemporaries considered him exceptionally able, and for that reason encouraged him in the project which survives as the *Pensées*. Subsequent history has largely erased his scientific and technological reputation, because progress in these fields must by definition continually leave behind the earlier steps in an endless process, but his solid success there owed nothing to the posthumous *Pensées*. Some otherwise intelligent critics, right up to our own time, have treated the *Pensées* as a betrayal of reason and science, a break and an aberration in a brilliant career. Others, less committed to the cause of rationalism, have none the less marked a discontinuity in Pascal's life without necessarily deploring it. The simple fact is that Pascal's very unusual life forms a coherent whole and that the *Pensées* derive from that life, as they could from no other, while drawing together its disparate threads.

If Pascal has proved to be a man for all seasons, it is because his life was shaped at every point by the peculiar pressures and tensions of the age in which he lived, when received ideas were being challenged on all sides by the advance of science, political and social change and religious controversy. The range of his work and experience is astonishingly wide, and makes up in intensity what it lacks in quantity. The specificity of this experience is further enhanced by his particular family situation, and by his precarious health. He could not, if he had wanted to, have stood aside from the realities of life; he did not even attempt to create an ivory tower of intellectual or literary detachment. It may be going a little too far to speak of the universality of his appeal, but even by crude commercial criteria he remains a bestseller. This is surely so because every reader, even when exasperated, must recognise in Pascal a man as deeply involved in the human predicament as those for whom he writes. The best way to understand him is to trace the course of his life and the stages by which he came to define his, and our, predicament in the striking terms of the *Pensées*.

Blaise Pascal was born on 19 June 1623 at Clermont (now Clermont-Ferrand) in Auvergne. His father, Etienne, was a successful lawyer of thirty-five, doing well in a traditionally prosperous profession. Only three years later, Etienne lost his wife Antoinette, of whom we know very little, and found himself responsible for two daughters, Gilberte and the infant Jacqueline, as well as for Blaise, apparently a sickly child. The effect of being brought up without a mother, an only son between an older and a younger sister, condemned moreover to indifferent health, would have been considerable for anyone, and seems to have marked Blaise's affective development permanently, in that he was always upset by displays of emotion in others. A further decisive element in the boy's upbringing was his father's insistence on educating him at home, partly to spare a delicate child the rough and tumble of school life, and partly because Etienne was an accomplished mathematician, as well as a lawyer, and thought, probably with reason, that he could teach his son as effectively as any schoolmaster. When the family moved to Paris in 1631, Etienne gave up all official duties and had time to concentrate on his self-appointed educational task.

From 1631 until 1640, when the family left for Rouen, Pascal pursued a course of education under his father's supervision which gave him a sound grounding in Latin, Greek, mathematics and science. Also important were the people he met through his father, united by a common interest in mathematics and science. Descartes (1596–1650) had already gone to live in Holland to escape the importunities of Paris salon society, but he had to come back from time to time, and his unofficial agent, the Minim Friar Père Mersenne, belonged to the same circle as Etienne Pascal. The publication in 1637 of Descartes' *Discourse on Method*, with the accompanying essays on optics, meteors and geometry, for the first time made available in French such technical subjects to the voracious and growing public of amateurs. The Cartesian (Descartes') revolution, for the barricades of traditional philosophy had never before been so rudely assaulted, thus came in time for the youthful Pascal to take it in and, in due course, challenge it in direct confrontation.

Posterity has dealt less generously with the resident Parisian members of the Mersenne circle, but in their own day Robcrval, Desargues and Fermat were the most famous mathematicians in France. All, in their turn, respected the precocious genius of their friend's young son, and whatever Blaise may have missed by not going to school, he did not lack praise and encouragement from acknowledged masters. It is easy for those of us who have failed to penetrate the mysteries of mathematics to see an almost magical gift in those who effortlessly do so, and this no doubt accounts for Gilberte's story of her brother's discovery of

Pythagoras' theorem by do-it-yourself methods when he was about twelve. His attested performance not many years later is more impressive than any dubious myth.

The Académie Française, founded by Richelieu in 1635, was essentially charged, as it still is, with literary and linguistic questions, and until the foundation of the Académie des Sciences by Colbert in 1666 provided an official forum, such informal groups as the scientific academy formed round Mersenne played the important role of discussing and diffusing problems and discoveries in the field of science. The Renaissance had aroused interest in all ancient writers, but with the partial exception of astronomy (inextricably linked to its detriment with astrology) and medicine (equally tainted by superstition), scientific subjects were regarded as occult mysteries rather than legitimate fields for systematic research, and no clear picture of the material world emerged from the welter of qualities, accidents, hierarchies and other terms of medieval science. Men like Leonardo and Copernicus won nothing like general acceptance. By the time Descartes came to write (and Pascal first heard discussion of the new ideas), alchemists, astrologers and quack doctors no longer dominated the scene. On the one hand, technical advances produced enormously improved instruments, like the telescope and microscope, whilst on the other, advances in mathematics made possible, and then essential, the replacement of mystery by calculation. The practical utility of science and mathematics for architecture, navigation, warfare and much else was soon appreciated, but there was also an insatiable curiosity to know more about man himself and the world around him. The advertised aim, for instance, of Descartes' method was to 'make us masters and possessors of nature', and the characteristic intellectual arrogance of the sixteenth century now extended beyond man's supremacy over other creatures and belief in his moral autonomy to the ambition to control his whole environment. Almost all of the Mersenne circle were amateurs, but in the seventeenth century it was educated men of independent means who were largely responsible for the major achievements in both arts and sciences. The age of the professional was yet to come, and the work of gifted amateurs must not be seen as a mere hobby. The relevance, then, of these years in Paris to Pascal's attitude and development is crucial.

Towards the end of their stay in Paris, the Pascal family made direct and disagreeable contact with another major fact of contemporary life: the absolute power exercised by Cardinal Richelieu. He had been effective ruler of France since 1624, and by ensuring the stability of Louis XIII's throne remained in power until his death in 1642, a few months before that of his royal master. It must not be forgotten that the most bloody war in French history had ended only in 1594, with Henri IV's entry into Paris, after intermittent hostilities lasting some thirty years, and that both Henri IV, in 1610, and his predecessor, Henri III, in 1589, had died at an assassin's hand. The first years of Louis XIII's minority were not auspicious, and when Richelieu became Minister in 1624, the need and desire of most Frenchmen was for law and order. The Thirty Years War (1618–48), Huguenot revolts, countless conspiracies by disgruntled nobles and periodic popular uprisings against crushing taxes made Richelieu rule with a very tight rein.

When, in 1638, Étienne Pascal joined a vocal demonstration against government action in suspending payment on a loan from which much of his income derived, Richelieu was greatly displeased. Étienne Pascal had to flee for a time to Auvergne, and it was only the winning ways of young Jacqueline, something of an actress and a poet, that secured his Eminence's pardon some months later. The immediate consequence of this episode was Richelieu's nomination of Étienne Pascal to be in charge of taxes at Rouen, where civil commotion had erupted into violence in protest against fiscal exactions. The appointment marked a return to favour, but at a price. By early 1640, when the Pascals moved to Rouen, Blaise had at any rate some direct experience of political reality, and Étienne's narrow escape from imprisonment was an object lesson not to be forgotten.

At Rouen, Blaise soon began the career for which his unorthodox education had prepared him. In 1640 he published a little treatise on conic sections (projective geometry). In 1642 he invented a calculating machine, and by 1644 a Rouen craftsman under his supervision had actually built the first of a small number of machines, all of which worked. In the circumstances of the age the production of working models is no less remarkable than the initial idea. By 1646 he had begun work on the problem of the vacuum, which was to win him public renown, and incidentally lead to his first clash with the Jesuits. These first fruits of his genius show a remarkable combination of purely intellectual and solidly practical qualities, quite exceptionally directed to an experimental method still in its infancy.

In 1646, however, a quite new element came into his life, sowing the seeds of an incalculable harvest. Following an injury to his leg, Étienne Pascal was treated by two brothers, local gentlemen who were amateur bonesetters. They were also Jansenists, practising their art, indeed, for charitable reasons connected with their faith. In the course of a stay, which eventually lasted three months, they converted the whole family, who placed themselves under the direction of a local priest of the same sympathies, M. Guillebert.

It is not easy to tell the precise effect upon Blaise of this first conversion, if only because we know virtually nothing of his spiritual dispositions before it. There was no question of joining another Church, or body within the Church, and no new credal expression. Jansenism at this stage was much more a way of life: practical works of charity (like the bonesetting) as against pious exercises, a conscious as against a mechanical sacramental discipline with regard to communion and confession, a deeper personal prayer life, an awareness of man's wretchedness and dependence on divine grace as against comfortable optimism and reliance on human means for salvation.

In these early days the impetus behind the Jansenist movement still came from Jean Duvergier de Hauranne, always known as the abbé Saint-Cyran, from the abbey of which he was titular and absent head, who had died in 1643 and had been spiritual director of the nuns at Port-Royal. Many years before, Saint-Cyran and the Fleming Cornelius Jansen had been fellow students at Louvain. There they had begun discussions, later carried on by correspondence over many years, about the means by which the Catholic Church could be brought back on course after what they saw as the disastrously man-centred theology of the

Counter-Reformation had swung it into moral laxity and spiritual tepidity. The Reformers, Luther, Calvin and others, had laid so much emphasis on man's helplessly sinful nature that it was inevitable that reaction should go the other way. The sixteenth-century Spanish Jesuit Molina gave his name to a theology of grace, Molinism, championed by his order and favoured by many 'modern' theologians outside it. Saint-Cyran and Jansen decided that the only remedy against this new man-centred theology lay in the Fathers of the Church, notably St Augustine, the great doctor of grace, and ironically a source to which Luther also appealed. Jansen worked away at a huge book on Augustine, but died in 1638 before it could be published, not long after becoming Bishop of Ypres; while Saint-Cyran was languishing in the Bastille from 1636, after a political disagreement with Richelieu. The nuns and others under his spiritual direction were rarely theologians, and men like Guillebert and the bonesetters stood for the simple kind of religion described above. In 1640, the year the Pascals moved to Rouen, Bishop Jansen's posthumous work was published as *Augustinus*, and quite coincidentally the Jesuits issued a volume of rhapsodical self-congratulations on their Society's first centenary. Two years later, in 1642, Saint-Cyran was released from the Bastille on Richelieu's death, but himself died in 1643. His place as leader of what they themselves called the Augustinians was taken by the Sorbonne theologian, Antoine Arnauld. Quite soon a major dispute began, in which Arnauld found himself defending Jansen's book against an increasingly violent campaign led by the Jesuits, who naturally called their opponents Jansenists.

As far as Pascal himself was concerned, the main effect of the first conversion seems to have been an acknowledgement of a new, more demanding, set of spiritual values, a more conscientious practice of the faith without any specific commitment to a way of life essentially different from that which he was already leading. His sister Jacqueline, however, soon felt the call of the cloister, and wanted to join the nuns at Port-Royal, where two of Arnauld's sisters successively ruled as abbess. The high point of her life up till then had been a meeting with Pierre Corneille, then at the height of his theatrical reputation, in his native Rouen, and to see her forsake her previous devotion to poetry, drama and social elegance for the inner life of the spirit cannot have failed to affect her brother, particularly as Gilberte had now married and gone to live in Auvergne. All in all, Blaise may at this stage be said to have seen the light by which he thenceforth judged spiritual questions, but he had not yet found or acknowledged his spiritual way.

In 1647 Blaise fell ill, perhaps through overwork, and he and Jacqueline moved to Paris, to be followed next year by their father. In September 1647 Pascal, while ill in bed, had two meetings with Descartes, but impressions were not favourable on either side. At about the same time Blaise made his first, rather unsatisfactory, contact with Port-Royal, while Jacqueline met vigorous opposition from her father to her plan to become a nun. Meanwhile, the series of experiments on the vacuum continued, and by 1651 Blaise was able to write a treatise on the whole subject. Shortly afterwards, in September, Étienne Pascal died, and Jacqueline waited barely three months before fulfilling her desire to enter the community of Port-Royal (in Paris). From then on, January 1652, Blaise was free, alone and of independent means.

The next few years form a confusing, and not very happy, period in Pascal's life. There were the inevitable problems arising out of his father's will, and there was a disagreement, at times acrimonious, over the precise terms of the financial settlement (the so-called 'dowry') of Jacqueline. He was involved in a social round, frivolous, no doubt, but probably innocuous, which must have been unsettling for an eligible young bachelor, deprived within the space of a few months of his father and the sister who had looked after them both. There were items on the credit side, however: his growing friendship with the young duc de Roannez and Charlotte, his younger sister, continuing successful work on science and mathematics, the lively intellectual and cultural life of Paris after the provincialism of Rouen. But in this so-called 'worldly' period Pascal seems temporarily to have lost his bearings, even if he was far from losing his head. He must have been asking himself questions about his future direction, but no conclusive answer had yet appeared.

Quite suddenly, on the night of 23 November 1654, he had an experience, a record of which survives in his own hand, which decisively and immediately determined the course of his remaining years. The exact nature of this second conversion is not in doubt, since the whole of Pascal's subsequent life reflects it, but it does not mark the clean break with previous occupations that some critics have claimed to see.

Essentially what happened was that Pascal at last felt able to overcome the obstacles to a full and committed love of God through Christ. He recognised these obstacles as being above all pride, especially intellectual pride, and selfishness, such as had caused his resentment at Jacqueline's fulfilment of her vocation at his expense, as he saw it. On that night he felt at last reconciled with Christ and resolved thenceforth to give himself wholeheartedly to the service of God and others. The spark of 1646 had become a consuming fire.

After Christmas, in January 1655, he went to Port-Royal-des-Champs, not far from Versailles (the original home of the nuns to which some of them had recently returned from Paris) for some weeks, to make a retreat with the solitaries, 'les Messieurs', who lived there in an informal, quasi-monastic community. He put himself under the direction of M. Singlin, and had important conversations with M. de Saci, a record of which survives. He embarked on serious spiritual reading and a way of life approved by his director. Significantly, in April 1655 he joined his friend Roannez and several others in a scheme for reclaiming marshland in Poitou, where Roannez had vast estates, thus allying technological skill and good works for the benefit of local people. It is true that for a time he did no work of consequence in mathematics or science, but he was exceptionally involved in theological problems, which demanded a lot of preparation for a beginner like himself. There is no evidence at all that he even thought of abandoning all those activities to which he owed a reputation, which his new friends at Port-Royal found most useful for their cause.

In January 1656, Pascal was once more making a retreat at Port-Royal when the situation of Arnauld, threatened with imminent censure by the Sorbonne (the Faculty of Theology at

Paris of which he was a member) at the conclusion of protracted
disputes over *Augustinus*, prompted Arnauld's friends to beg
their recent recruit to lend his help. The result was the series of
Provincial Letters (see p. 32), which finally numbered eighteen
and came to an end in March 1657. During this frantically busy
and genuinely dangerous time, Pascal also started work on a
treatise on miracles, following the cure of his niece, Jacqueline
Périer, whose eye was healed of a longstanding fistula after contact with a relic of the Holy Thorn (supposedly part of the
Crown of Thorns of the Passion) kept at Port-Royal. To 1656
also belong an important series of letters to the duc and Charlotte
de Roannez of spiritual direction.

Once involved in the Jansenists' struggle for survival, Pascal
went on publishing theological and polemical works throughout
1657 and 1658, and at some time in 1657 began thinking about an
Apology for the Christian Religion, of which the *Pensées* represent all that he had time to complete. This intense religious
activity did not prevent him promoting an international competition to solve the problem of the cycloid (or 'roulette', that is,
the path traced by a peg, fixed on the circumference of a moving
wheel), a geometrical puzzle with no practical application, but
requiring great technical ingenuity for its solution. By the beginning of 1659 Pascal's health had deteriorated so much that he
could only work for brief periods, but he continued as best he
could with the composition of his *Apology*. It was only at this
point, after he had judged himself (pseudonymously) the winner
of the cycloid competition, that he gave up mathematics and
science, but this was, beyond all doubt, for reasons of health, not
at all because of his conversion.

Momentary improvements in his health enabled Pascal to go to
Auvergne in 1660 to take the waters, and to go on writing, among
other things, three brief but impressive essays *On the Noble Estate*,
eventually published in edited form by Pierre Nicole, a Port-
Royal stalwart. In October 1661, Jacqueline died at Port-Royal,
worn out and reputedly broken-hearted at the relentless per-
secution to which the community and their supporters had been
subjected. The final blow had been an edict in April 1661 demanding signature of unconditional acceptance of the judgement

regarding Arnauld and the *Augustinus*. Pascal, as a layman, was not personally affected by the edict, but disagreed with Port-Royal's capitulation.

The last twelve months of Pascal's life were dark with sickness and grief, but in March 1662, by now very ill (with a condition never properly diagnosed), he saw the fulfilment of another of his projects, the one perhaps with the greatest social and practical consequences: a bus service, 'coaches at 5 sous', was inaugurated under his direction from the Porte Saint-Antoine (near the Bastille) to the Luxembourg, and the profits assigned to the relief of the poor. Like the adding machine at the beginning of his career, this project was easier to conceive than to execute, and bears fitting testimony to the practical side of Pascal's genius.

At the end of June 1662, Pascal was so ill that he moved in with his sister Gilberte, now installed in Paris, and there, in the heart of the Latin Quarter, he died in physical distress but spiritual serenity on 19 August 1662. He was buried in the parish church of Saint-Étienne-du-Mont, where his memorial can still be seen, next to what is now the Panthéon.

The reputation he enjoyed at his death was enormous, but did not correspond at all to that which survives today. Leading mathematicians and scientists like Fermat and Huyghens respected him as an outstanding member of the intellectual community, as well as a personal friend. Neither they, however, nor such others as Christopher Wren, who was interested in the cycloid problem, or Leibniz, to whom some of Pascal's papers were sent later, had much, if any, interest in his literary and religious work (if indeed they knew it). The peasants of Poitou and the passengers of the first Paris transport service knew of him, if at all, as someone who had contributed to their material welfare. In the salons, and soon in an international public, the *PLs* were much admired (the English translation appeared only months after the original) as a brilliant piece of polemic, and the Jesuits of course knew and bitterly resented the satirical masterpiece, but the secrecy which had been necessary for security reasons meant that the author's identity was not at all widely known in his lifetime.

Only his family and the inner circle of his friends inside and outside Port-Royal even knew about the uncompleted *Apology*, and when a much-edited version appeared in 1670 it caused nothing like the excitement occasioned by the *PLs*. For this inner circle, Pascal was a holy man, perhaps a saint, and scraps of autograph material by him were sought and treasured as relics, contributing thereby not a little to the problems of modern scholars. Above all, for these people Pascal was the spokesman for their own threatened and beleaguered form of Catholic Christianity, and these 'friends of truth', as the Jansenists liked to call themselves, were not the best sponsors for a work of general appeal. It is really only since the last century that the *Pensées* have been studied and edited seriously, and appreciated by a wider public, and only in the last forty years that any true picture of the work, with an edition respecting Pascal's actual composition, has been available.

Nowadays the scientific and mathematical work is of interest only to the historians of those fields, the *PLs* are read by students of literature and religion as a superbly written record of past conflicts, and only the *Pensées* enjoy a wide readership which shows no signs of shrinking. It is absolutely certain that the present estimate of his achievement is what Pascal would have wished. Neither his enemies nor his friends have been able to hide his light.

2 Science and technology

Pascal's work on science, including mathematics, and in technology is important for the results he achieved, but it also illustrates aspects of his character and reveals patterns of thought which were to develop in a completely different context after his conversion.

In a dedicatory letter (1645) to the Chancellor, Séguier, Pascal introduced a model of his calculating machine with an explicit reference to the laborious methods of calculation involved in helping his father work out fiscal problems. Seeing the need for a labour-saving device, he worked out a theory and then proceeded to build a machine. Valid claims have been made for earlier pioneers in this field, but in this, his first such venture, Pascal (almost certainly ignorant of his predecessors) excelled as he so often did later by the clarity of his thought and rigorous practicality of execution.

The land reclamation project in Poitou was not his idea, but is important for correcting the very widespread impression that Jansenists held aloof from material affairs. Apart from the solitaries, who lived a monastic life without vows, most Jansenist laymen did not withdraw from the world. On the contrary, like Quakers and Nonconformists in England, they regarded it as their Christian duty to do good works. In the case of Roannez, he and his associates (not all of whom were, in fact, Jansenists) were enthusiastic supporters of various technological innovations, including canal navigation and a new form of two-wheeled carriage, as well as land reclamation. Honest and constructive work, backed by financial and technical resources, appealed to such men as a very proper use of human talents.

Rather the same is true of the transport project. It was unquestionably a public utility, but was not, nevertheless, available to workmen, soldiers and liveried servants, whose presence would surely have deterred its mainly bourgeois (and female) users. Even with such limitations it met a need, and eventually three lines were running, until in 1679 the service ceased to be profitable and had to close. Social conscience played a part in this enterprise, but the organisation and vision needed to bring it to fruition were very much Pascal's contribution, made when he was extremely ill.

The cycloid affair was only the last of a whole series of scientific activities, some of which have been lost, which demonstrate not only Pascal's great technical competence, but also his intellectual pride. The quite considerable extant material connected with the problem, its solution and entries for the competition shows that as late as 1658, four years after his conversion, Pascal had not succeeded in exorcising this pride, amounting to arrogance, which his precocious exploits as a boy had made his besetting sin. It was one thing for Descartes to treat critics and rivals with high-handed disdain: his private vision (of November 1654) had convinced him that he had a unique prophetic mission to reveal the truth; but it was quite another for Pascal, committed to abasement of the self since his conversion experience, to show no trace of humility (and more than a hint of sharp practice) in demonstrating his superiority as a mathematician. This tension between the intellectual and the spiritual man is a basic ingredient of the *Pensées*.

Of his mathematical works, the most solid is to do with what is now called probability theory. Typically, his interest in the subject was first aroused by a purely practical problem. One of his friends, an assiduous gambler, but no mathematician, asked him to work out an equitable distribution of stakes between participants in a game interrupted before its conclusion. The problem was obviously not new, and solutions had been propounded before, but Pascal's achievement was to solve it with greater simplicity and elegance than others, and above all to draw from the solution to a particular problem a multiplicity of wide-ranging conclusions. The details are to be found in correspondence with the Toulouse mathematician Fermat in 1654, and in some printed papers dating from about the same time, but not published until after Pascal's death.

Pascal begins with a simple example. Two players have agreed to play dice until one wins three throws. Each has put in 32 pistoles, a substantial sum; one has won two throws, his opponent one. At the fourth throw the first either wins, thus winning all the money (64 pistoles), or his opponent wins, in which case, if the game is interrupted at that point, there is a draw and each takes away his original stake of 32 pistoles. Should they agree not to play this fourth throw, the first player can rightfully claim the 32 pistoles which would be his even if he lost and, the chances of winning and losing being equal, the remaining 32 should be divided in half, 16 going to each, so that one player ends with 48 and the other with 16. The demonstration continues through a whole range of game situations, and can be adapted for any number of players, dice or any other factor, and in each case Pascal establishes by referring back to his original example the proper distribution of money at any stage of an interrupted game.

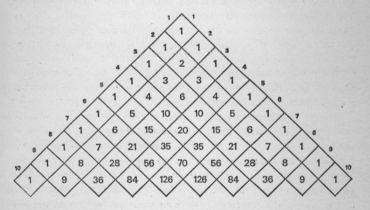

A simple diagram accompanied Pascal's letter, but soon afterwards he expanded this into what is still called Pascal's, or the Arithmetical, Triangle. Though he was by no means the first to produce such a figure, he does not seem to have known about his predecessors, and in any case differs from them in the wide variety of conclusions he was able to draw from the triangle, which they never even suspected. It will be seen that the construction of the figure is extremely simple: each square in the outermost diagonal rows contains the number 1; next comes the simple progression 1, 2, 3, 4 . . . ; thereafter the sequences of numbers (symmetrical diagonal rows are identical in content) are constructed by taking the preceding number and adding to it the sum of all the previous numbers in the diagonal row at right angles to the diagonal being constructed. Apart from the original gambling problem, one of the first (and today the best known) conclusions Pascal drew from this figure concerns binomial coefficients, that is the elements of such an expression as $(a+b)^2$ written out in full. For technical reasons, this is done by taking the horizontal row joining the two reference numbers (the numbers outside the matrix of squares) corresponding to the power required plus 1. Thus horizontal 3 runs through the squares containing the numbers which give the coefficients of $(a+b)^2$, namely $1(a^2)+2(ab)+1(b^2)$, horizontal 4 performs the same function for $(a+b)^3$, namely $1(a^3)+3(a^2b)+3(ab^2)+1(b^3)$, and so on.

A further consequence is similar, and of general application, whether the problem concerns throws of a dice, selecting x objects from a total of y, or any other form of chance. Again selecting the horizontal corresponding to the number required plus 1, in a game of heads and tails 3 throws (horizontal 4) offers a total of 8 chances, composed of $1(3 \text{ heads})+3(2 \text{ heads}, 1 \text{ tail})+3(2 \text{ tails}, 1 \text{ head})+1(3 \text{ tails})$. Thus the chance can be expressed as a fraction of which the denominator is the sum of the numbers running along a given horizontal and the numerator the number corresponding to a particular result, so that the chance of throwing 3 heads in succession is 1/8, 4 heads in succession 1/16, and so on for the whole range of possibilities.

The figure of the triangle provided a convenient visual aid, but of course its application to very large numbers could be effected through formulae without recourse to a diagram. Experts are not in agreement as to whether Pascal was on the track of the calculus theory, discovered independently, and more or less simultaneously, by Newton and Leibniz some twenty-five years after his death, but all that can be said with certainty is that mathematicians recognise that Pascal used methods both in his solution of the cycloid problem and in developing the possibilities presented by the Arithmetical Triangle which could logically be extended to the discovery of calculus. Nowadays, when even quite young children are taught calculus, it is hard to appreciate how distinguished and advanced Pascal's work appeared in his own day.

He himself attached particular importance to what he called 'the mathematics of chance', the precursor of statistical method and probability theory. Perhaps his best known application of this method is to be found in the *Pensées* (418) in the so-called 'Wager', where the unbeliever is invited to wager for or against God's existence (and thus of eternal life) on the basis of a maximum possible gain (infinite life in heaven) and a maximum possible loss (free use of a finite life on earth) in one case, and the reverse in the other.

In one way or another all this work in science and mathematics can be seen as relevant to Pascal's personal development and reputation. The major remaining work, that on the vacuum, is of more direct importance for revealing the attitudes and habits of mind he had already acquired in scientific work before they were transformed by being set in a religious context.

While still at Rouen, Pascal heard of the experiments conducted by the Florentine Torricelli in 1644, and in 1646 with his father's friend, the fortress engineer Pierre Petit, began a series of investigations and experiments extending until 1651. Pascal's projected treatise on the vacuum (*Traité du vide*) never materialised, but two posthumously published papers on barometric pressure (*l'Équilibre des liqueurs*) and the hydraulic press (*La Pesanteur de la masse d'air*) came out in 1663. The research itself, the controversy it aroused and Pascal's fundamental rethinking of scientific method are all equally characteristic and significant of the man and his role.

In 1644 Torricelli, a disciple of Galileo, showed that when a tube filled with mercury and open at one end was up-ended into a bath of mercury, it lost enough mercury from the top, enclosed, end to give the impression of an empty space, a vacuum, between the glass and the top level of mercury. Variations of the experiment, involving water and mercury, were observed to produce similar results. The interesting consequences of this phenomenon for hydraulics and the barometer were of infinitely less moment to Pascal's contemporaries than the antecedent problem of the apparent vacuum. It is hard to think of any modern parallel to the shiver of horror engendered by the mere suggestion to a man of the seventeenth century that a vacuum could effortlessly exist and be maintained; a materialist forced to admit irrefutable evidence of life after death might offer a fair analogy, but science, and science fiction, have accustomed us to the idea of the impossible in the physical universe. There were two completely different kinds of opposition to accepting the vacuum: there were the traditionalists, who, despite great progress in detail, still went back to Aristotle, via medieval Scholasticism, for the basic principles of physics, and there were the Cartesians, who rejected all ancient authority but proved by the pure, irresistible light of reason that a vacuum was simply impossible. The very fact that a young man of twenty-three, with no academic credentials whatever, was prepared to question both the authority of the ancients and that of the most illustrious modern tells us much about Pascal's character, and the further fact that he succeeded explains much of his later career.

The magic formula 'nature abhors a vacuum' and the belief that only the most strenuous efforts can produce one for a fleeting moment before nature reasserts her power, had exactly the same inhibiting force as belief in the earth as the centre of the universe. Galileo, condemned while Pascal was still a child, could not be stopped from testing a hypothesis incompatible with geocentric dogma, and fell foul of the Inquisition for proving that dogma wrong. Pascal, less dangerously, resolved to test nature's reputed abhorrence of the vacuum, and finding no alternative hypothesis to fit the facts, announced to the world, in 1647, that pending further discoveries it must be assumed that what appeared to be a vacuum was precisely that. Moreover, he posited, nature offered not even token resistance to its continued existence. By an irony of history, the cause of traditional science was championed by a Jesuit, invitingly named Père Noël, Rector of the Jesuits' prestigious college in Paris (Collège de Clermont, later Louis-le-Grand). The kindly tone of Noël's letter, tolerantly pointing out the error of his ways to this impetuous youth, with deferential references to the wisdom transmitted over two thousand years, provoked a reply from Pascal which combined feline courtesy with devastating irony.

The dispute continued, with further letters from Noël, from Pascal's father on behalf of his son and from others, but the decisive report of the Puy-de-Dôme experiments deprived the opposition of all arguments save that of authority. The account of the experiment, conducted by Pascal's brother-in-law Florin Périer, shows a genuine desire to find the truth, check all possible factors affecting it and set out in the simplest terms what had actually been observed. It was left to Pascal himself to draw the consequences from the experiment, both theoretical and practical. Nothing could be more straightforward than the sober recital of facts, nothing less convincing than the verbal intricacy with which Noël sought to explain away the phenomena observed.

It is worth recording the bare facts of the great experiment. Having waited for some weeks for favourable weather, Périer assembled his team in a convent garden in the town of Clermont. Two identical tubes were tested together in the same mercury bath, and the reading at successive immersions duly noted by the group assembled, amongst which were respected clergy, lawyers and doctors. It was established that no variation occurred between the two tubes. A priest was left in the garden with one of the tubes, instructed to note whether the reading changed at any time during the day. Meanwhile, the others set off up the mountain of Puy-de-Dôme, and on its summit (1465 metres) took readings in the open, under cover, and in the different weather conditions experienced on a very changeable day. Halfway down they did the same, and on their return checked their tube once more against the control, which of course had not changed. The readings were accurate, though Périer apologises for the less accurate calculation of altitude, and the now familiar facts of atmospheric pressure established clearly and without doubt.

There remained the question of the vacuum; what filled the tube between the top of the column of mercury and the end of the tube? The standard solution spoke of very thin air or very subtle or refined particles of mercury, but never offered any explanation of how the mercury could once more rise to the top of the tube with no apparent resistance from the tenuous material whose location it was reoccupying. For Pascal's purposes, empty space in the tube was a vacuum, for his opponents it could not be, though they could not prove it scientifically. Towards the end of the controversy, Noël added to his Aristotelian arguments one from the diametrically opposed system of Descartes, showing once more that desperation rather than scientific detachment moved him.

Descartes' position was completely different from that of the traditionalists. When they came up against a problem they simply invented a quality, a name to explain it. Thus they said that it was heaviness which made lead fall faster than a feather, whose distinctive quality was lightness; a vegetative life-principle (*anima*) made a tree grow, lack of one made stones inanimate. For them such qualities had real and absolute value. Descartes' great contribution to thought was to dismiss every one of these qualities, to unite the previously separate sciences of biology, physics, chemistry and the rest and explain the whole physical world in quantitative terms, that is, mathematically and mechanically, with the same laws applying throughout the world of matter in all its forms. To this end he defined matter simply as interchangeable with the geometrical co-ordinates, that is space, in which it was located. It therefore necessarily followed that empty space in Cartesian terms is a contradiction; where there is space there is matter and vice versa. The method by which Descartes arrived at this revolutionary conclusion was rigorously rationalistic and formulated *a priori*. He quite literally based his physics on metaphysics in advance of any observation, and went so far as to prove the law of inertia as a necessary consequence of certain equally necessary attributes of God, themselves established by the unaided light of reason.

It would be convenient if one could say who was right and who was wrong, but one of the great difficulties, then as now, is that the right answer held for the wrong reasons may inhibit discovery of the right reasons. Certainly if intellectual rigour, with insistence on a proper scientific method, are the pre-requisites for progress, Pascal wins against Noël and Descartes, whose absolute dogmatism prejudged all issues; but in modern, rather than seventeenth-century terms, the issue can be seen as less clear-cut. What Pascal had observed was a vacuum for all practical purposes (like modern vacuum jars) and he was right to insist that this high degree of vacuum requires no special force. He was right too, to say that until the material alleged to be in the apparently empty space was identified he would persist in treating it as non-existent. Current definitions of matter (recognising as matter, for instance, radio, light and other kinds of waves) and vastly improved measuring techniques would meet Pascal's challenge, and his use of the word vacuum, would have to be qualified with some very high percentage of vacuum. As for Descartes, his predilection for an essentially mathematical physics is much in favour today, but the metaphysical foundations were rejected almost before he was dead, and the physics did not survive much longer, being too rigid a system, and too simplistic, to match observed facts.

There is no point in trying to allot marks for Pascal and Descartes on this issue: each of them made an immense contribution to contemporary thought, but in the last analysis they represent permanent and irreconcilable poles in human thought. A clear and succinct picture of the issues at stake is drawn in the *Preface* to Pascal's unfinished, and lost, treatise on the vacuum.

This text is of crucial importance, though only a few pages long, as it was written in 1651, well before Pascal's conversion, and establishes an unbroken chain between his scientific and religious work by giving a first version of the theory of orders. Pascal begins with a statement to the effect that blind respect for the authority of the ancients (as much a legacy of Renaissance humanism as of medieval Scholasticism) is a major obstacle to intellectual progress. He goes on to make a capital distinction between different kinds of knowledge.

Those subjects in which the authority of antiquity is absolute include history, geography, law, languages and 'above all theology', since they all depend on human or divine institution, of which the original documents are the sole and sufficient source. Unexpectedly in a scientific work, he enlarges on the nature of theological truth, insisting that its principles are 'above nature and reason'. Descartes, notably in his *Meditations*, had claimed exactly the opposite, namely that the existence and nature of God can, and should, be proved by purely rational means.

The second category of subjects falls into the domain of 'the senses or reasoning' (reason being the faculty, reasoning the process, ratiocination) and includes geometry, arithmetic, music (regarded here as a scientific rather than an aesthetic study), architecture and experimental sciences. In all these fields progress is necessary, and unending, each generation handing on its store of knowledge to be increased by the next.

There follows a paragraph to remind us that from the time of his first conversion in 1646, Pascal shared the hostility of all Jansenists to the theological novelties introduced and defended above all by the Jesuits. Père Noël may have clashed with Pascal on a purely scientific issue, but he was a Jesuit with standards in theology inseparable in Pascal's mind from his impertinence in science. Pascal combines an attack on those who cite authority as the only proof in physics with those who wickedly 'use reasoning alone in theology instead of the authority of the Scriptures and the Fathers', and goes on to speak of the need to 'confound the insolence of those who boldly proclaim novelties in theology'. The reference was unmistakable, and applicable as much to Descartes, educated by the Jesuits at La Flèche, with his rational theology, as to his masters with their sixteenth-century theology of grace and their constantly evolving moral theology. Tone and attitude here anticipate the *PLs*, and it is evident that more than scientific truth is at stake.

Returning for the rest of the *Preface* to science, Pascal dwells on the notion of progress and the importance of experiment, concluding with a fundamental observation which marks his disagreement with both Descartes and the traditionalists: 'in all matters where the proof lies in experiments and not in demonstrations, no universal assertion can be made except by general enumeration of all the different parts or cases'. Thus at any given moment such statements as one claiming that a diamond is the hardest of bodies must be understood with the addition of the proviso 'of all the bodies we know'. It necessarily follows that Pascal subjected his own findings about the vacuum to the same proviso, and would gladly have devised fresh experiments to deal with fresh techniques and discoveries.

A point too often missed in comments on this text is that the appeal to authority in, for instance, theology, is contrasted with two, not just one, appeals to the human faculties of the senses *or* reason. Experimental observation is a matter for the senses, its interpretation (and the devising of further experiments) a matter for reason. Descartes erred, in Pascal's view, by dogmatically setting down physical laws on the basis of pure reason, uncorroborated by the senses, which Descartes always deeply distrusted. For Pascal, all explanation of the physical world must derive from sense observation, the only contact we have with that world, in turn analysed by reason; for Descartes all the basic laws of nature are 'imprinted in our minds' and should in the first instance be examined there, not in the world outside. In such areas as mathematics and logic, reason alone is the guide – we cannot with the senses perceive perfect circles or straight lines – but Pascal absolutely rejected the idea that reason alone was the way to truth in theology or the physical sciences.

The plain message of the *Preface* is that there are three ways to knowledge, or orders, depending on the subject under investigation, and that the appeal to authority is as misguided in physics as the appeal to reason or senses in theology. One does not listen to a rose, or smell a symphony, and although Pascal does not yet use the word 'order', this is what he already saw in 1651. He saw, moreover, that each order – authority, reason, senses – is autonomous in its own domain and not arranged in a hierarchy of excellence. At this stage appropriateness is the only criterion for judging between orders in a given context.

As a footnote to what has just been said, it is worth recording that Descartes, though fully aware of the importance of experiment for eliminating false hypotheses, was so mesmerised by his *a priori* reasoning that he claimed to have refuted *by experiment* the English doctor William Harvey's recently published theory of the circulation of the blood. Keen enough to get up early in the morning to watch beasts being cut up in the Amsterdam abattoirs, he could still maintain, with perfect logic, that the body of a man, like that of any other animal, was an internal combustion engine, fired by the exceptional heat of the heart vaporising and circulating the blood. One cannot imagine Pascal thus preferring logic to observation and common sense.

Several years later, after his conversion, Pascal set down some thoughts on different types of mind. One version of these can be found in the two incomplete texts, posthumously published (written about 1657–8) and probably intended as prefaces to textbooks for use in the schools run at Port-Royal (where Racine, among others, was a pupil). Other substantial parts are published as fragments in modern editions of the *Pensées*, though they never belonged to the apologetic project. The longer texts are entitled *De l'esprit géométrique* (The mathematical mind) and *De l'art de persuader* (The art of persuasion). The former is particularly interesting in the present context since it contains a distinction between different types of reasoning directly relevant to Pascal's own use of scientific method, but the crucial distinction is best put in *Pensées* 511 and 512. The two types of mind are defined in 512 as 'mathematical' and 'intuitive' (*géométrique, fin*) and while 511 concludes by saying that it is possible to have one without the other, it is clear that Pascal regarded a combination of the two as best.

At first (511) he distinguishes between the 'powerful and precise mind' going 'rapidly and deeply into the conclusions from principles' and 'breadth of mind', which 'can grasp a great number of principles and keep them distinct' and is 'the mathematical mind'. In the second fragment, however, he somewhat modifies this distinction:

mathematicians who are merely mathematicians reason soundly as long as everything is explained to them by definitions and principles, otherwise they are unsound and intolerable, because they reason soundly only from clearly defined principles. And intuitive minds which are merely intuitive lack the patience to go right into the first principles of speculative and imaginative matters which they have never seen in practice and are quite outside ordinary experience.

A further elucidation follows (513): 'Judgement is what goes with instinct (*sentiment*), just as knowledge goes with mind *(esprit).* Intuition falls to the lot of judgement, mathematics *(géométrie)* to that of mind.' He has already explained (512) that the principles of mathematics are obvious, but remote from ordinary usage, while for the intuitive mind

the principles are in ordinary usage and there for all to see. There is no need to turn our heads, or strain ourselves; it is only a question of good sight, but it must be good; for the principles are so intricate and numerous that it is almost impossible not to miss some. Now the omission of one principle can lead to error, and so one needs very clear sight to see all the principles, as well as an accurate mind to avoid drawing false conclusions from known principles.

The application of these last words to the Puy-de-Dôme experiment is instructive: the everyday principles involved comprised weather, time of day, altitude, purity of mercury and equipment and other factors. Only by devising an experiment which would omit the consequences of none of these could Pascal draw scientifically rigorous conclusions.

It will be seen that the purely intellectual function of the mathematical mind is here contrasted with the instinct or intuition with which it should ideally be associated. In fact the rather bald concept of authority, as seen in the *Preface*, had by 1657–8 become an inner, rather than an outer, order, represented by the word 'heart' *(coeur).* The treatise on persuasion written at that time makes the point neatly. Pascal begins by saying that men are always persuaded either through their intellect *(entendement)* or will, but specifically excludes divine truths. God alone, he says, can implant them, and 'he wants them to enter the mind from the heart, and not the heart from the mind, to humiliate that arrogant power of reasoning . . .'.

This is not the place to dwell further on distinctions involving religion, but enough has been said by now to show that at all times Pascal recognised three ways to truth and knowledge. Whether in a scientific or explicitly religious context he added a third term to the usual reason and senses (or mind and body), and variously defined it as the will that submits to authority, instinct, intuition or heart. The continuity of this triple division, so radically different from Descartes' dualism of mind and matter and the unchallenged supremacy of reason, is unmistakable and basic to an understanding of Pascal's life and thought. Throughout all his scientific work his ultimate criterion is 'submission to the facts', however inconvenient, and this basic attachment to concrete facts rather than abstract principles was to persist as a characteristic element of all his later work on religion.

3 Ethics and casuistry

The first literary fruit of Pascal's conversion of November 1654 is the conversation with M. de Saci, of which an edited version survives to give a sufficiently reliable account. Having by the fact of conversion turned his back on the world, Pascal was invited during his retreat at Port-Royal to describe to Saci (one of the solitaries, with a considerable reputation as a spiritual director) the values by which that world lived. It is highly significant that Pascal's talk says nothing of scientific or technological pursuits, but deals solely with the moral life. The humanism of the sixteenth-century Renaissance had been characterised by a general enthusiasm for Classical antiquity and especially for the moral systems developed by pagans. The attraction of an ethic independent of, but preferably compatible with, Christianity was peculiarly strong for men passionately searching for universal truths, applicable to all men as men and not conditional on their religious status.

The cult of pagan virtue, exemplified above all in the person of the Greek philosopher Socrates, led to all kinds of adjustments in existing categories such as, for example, the pagan and the Christian. One of the many solutions propounded for the awkward problem of the conspicuous virtue practised even unto death by a pre-Christian like Socrates was to enrol him as a kind of honorary Christian or, in the words of a very early Christian writer (Eusebius), 'a Greek Moses'. Other favoured solutions involved total separation of the moral and religious life, and in one form or another the problem is still alive in theological debate.

As far as Jansenists were concerned, pagan virtue was simply a contradiction in terms. Man's corrupt nature enabled him to *do* good only when aided by divine grace, and for Jansenists there was never any question of man *being* naturally good, or of becoming good by purely natural means. This, of course, was the very basis for the original reaction of Saint-Cyran and Jansen against the man-centred theology of the Jesuit Molina, and became the main issue in the quarrel with the Jesuits, who officially adopted such a theology in the seventeenth century. But at this stage in Pascal's religious development he was not at all deeply involved with theology, and his treatment of moral issues with Saci is that of a man of the world familar with philosophy but not at all a specialist or professional.

The views he chose for analysis and criticism are diametrically opposed, and represented the extreme alternatives of those who did not wholeheartedly follow the Gospel. Montaigne (1533–92, author of the *Essays*) is selected for his scepticism (or Pyrrhonism, as it should strictly be called, that is, suspension of judgement on all things); and Epictetus (a freed Greek slave, died *c.* A.D. 125) for his dogmatic Stoicism. Both were selected for their contemporary appeal to the *honnête homme* of polite society. The choice of antagonists is interesting in itself, but made more interesting by the fact that in all his later work Pascal continued to denounce Pyrrhonism and Stoicism as pre-eminent among false philosophies, almost ignoring Plato and Aristotle, who were immensely more distinguished among ancient philosophers, and attacking Descartes virtually always for his mechanistic view of the natural order, rather than for more fundamental elements of his ethics or metaphysics.

The influence of Montaigne on Pascal was deep and extensive, and by no means all negative, but it must be emphasised that for Pascal, as for Descartes, Montaigne was the arch exponent of scepticism. The hard-headed empiricism, the humane liberalism, the real personal courage which the modern reader finds in Montaigne, were totally eclipsed in the seventeenth century by the scepticism and fideism of which he was so engaging a spokesman. Pascal and Descartes were undoubtedly right in their own terms, different as they were from each other, to recognise in Montaigne a profoundly subversive influence on the minds and hearts of easy-going, civilised men. As for Epictetus, his little *Manual*, a mere thirty or forty pages of utmost simplicity in the existing French translations, was the ideal handbook for those of more heroic temper, and afforded a much more concise statement of practical Stoicism than could be found in, for example, Cicero and Seneca, universally revered as these authors were throughout

the sixteenth century. It was, incidentally, revulsion against
Stoicism which as much as anything else drove Montaigne into
what is called the sceptical crisis, when he struck a medal with
the inscription 'What do I know?', and wrote 'I suspend judgement' on the beams of his study.

Being on a small scale and with a limited objective, this
transcript in dialogue form of the conversation with Saci illustrates particularly well the way in which Pascal developed his
existing methodology and theory of orders to fit the requirements
of religious debate. This is the first instance of a technique he
constantly used in later years, by which existing categories are
shown inadequate for the solution of a given problem, usually by
selecting polar opposites which cancel each other out, so that a
new third term is introduced from outside to permit solution and
further progress. As set out by Pascal, Montaigne's argument is
as follows: man's besetting sin is arrogance, based on absurdly
inflated claims made for human reason, but the greatest of philosophers throughout history have never agreed amongst themselves, therefore the truth is not accessible, or rather not
recognisable, by the light of reason alone. Moreover, man's
vaunted superiority over animals does not stand up to investigation, since animals are stronger, kinder and perhaps even
wiser than men, and in any case the validity of reason (defined as
the faculty which distinguishes men from animals) as an instru-
ment for discerning truth is completely undermined by the unre-
liability of the senses, on which in the last analysis reason
depends. Therefore, says Montaigne, man should abandon arrogance for the humility appropriate to his true state. Thus far
Pascal agrees that Montaigne, and sceptics in general, can ad-
minister a salutary lesson to man, whose original sin persists in
all forms of intellectual pride.

Montaigne's conclusion, however, was quite unacceptable to
Pascal, who constantly denounced it as pernicious. Since
human reason is not capable of finding truth, moral or any other,
Montaigne thought that the best policy was simply not to worry,
to follow our inclinations, while prudently avoiding excess, and
rejoice in our ignorance. Montaigne's longest and most
influential essay, the *Apology for Raymond Sebond* (a fifteenth-

century Catalan theologian whom he had translated at his
father's request), admittedly asserted man's feebleness and helpless dependence on God, but made religious faith a purely pass-
ive acceptance of the Church's teaching. Man's very weakness
absolved him, in Montaigne's eyes, from the obligation to make
the smallest effort (for how could he know what was right or
wrong?) or even to be anxious about his future. This total divorce
of faith and reason (or judgement) was perhaps the most effective
way of surviving during the savage religious wars which dark-
ened nearly all of Montaigne's adult life, but fideism, as such
divorce is technically called, encouraged just that kind of easy-
going nonchalance, that urbane scepticism, which Pascal believed to be the most insidious enemy of religion.

If Montaigne's 'soft pillow' of ignorance infuriated Pascal, the
self-assurance of the Stoics seemed to him just as dangerous at
the opposite extreme. The moral system of the Stoics met a variety of needs in the sixteenth century, and continued to attract
admiration in the seventeenth, with its 'contempt for matters of
chance' and the belief that man's dignity lies in his power of
reason, by which he can and should acquire self-mastery. The
sublimity of the lives, and especially the deaths, of Stoics in antiquity, men like Cato and Brutus, writers like Seneca and Marcus
Aurelius and, overshadowing them all, Socrates, patron saint of
all Stoics, though he died before the Stoic school was formed; the
obvious affinity with Christian martyrs and heroic warriors; and
similar considerations, all made Stoicism the natural choice for
men of genuinely noble ideals. Stoicism was quite easily adapt-
able to Christianity (the translation of Epictetus used by Pascal
had in fact been made by a monk of a particularly strict order),
but Pascal was right to see that while the conduct of a Stoic
might be outwardly indistinguishable from that of a Christian
their motives must, in the last analysis, be strictly incompatible.

Pascal praises the teaching of Epictetus in so far as it con-
demns the passions and encourages detachment from all earthly
ties, even from family and friends. He naturally admires the
austerity and fortitude of Stoics, and approves their emphasis on
moral effort as against the limp self-indulgent heedlessness of
Montaigne. He stresses the basic tenet of Stoicism, whereby all

things come of God and should therefore be accepted by man as God's will, for good or ill, and that man's reason is fully adequate for the attainment of happiness. However, at this point Epictetus goes too far, and echoing the serpent in Eden instructs man that by right use of reason he can aspire to equality of wisdom and virtue (though not power) with God. This claim Pascal describes as diabolical arrogance, leading to such perversions as praise of suicide, common among the Stoics. After such an exposition of Stoicism, Montaigne's attack on reason (which follows it in Pascal's conversation) seems at first a wholesome and necessary corrective.

Pascal's summing-up gives a remarkable preview of one of the chief motifs of the *Pensées*. Epictetus, he says, recognises man's duties but not his moral impotence, and thus leads man to presumption; Montaigne recognises the impotence and not the duties, and so encourages cowardly inertia. Each establishes contrary truths and falsehoods, so that the two cancel each other out. The Gospels alone show how man's greatness and wretchedness can be reconciled, not, as with the two secular philosophers, within the same purely human nature, but by joining the weakness of that nature with the greatness conferred by grace, both united in the person of Christ. The inexorable march of Pascal's argument has the clarity of a mathematical demonstration, concluding almost with a conjuror's flourish when he shows that without introducing a new order, that of grace, the opposites can never be reconciled. The trick lies in taking as far as it can be taken the logic of the opponents' arguments, and suddenly revealing that not the steps but the premisses were wrong. Henceforth the intervention of the theory of orders is an almost invariable feature of Pascal's dialectic, forcing the opponent to admit that human reason can go no further, before triumphantly proclaiming that the answer must therefore lie outside human reason.

Because Descartes' moral system was largely a variation on Stoicism, the attack on Epictetus is partly applicable to him, and it is relevant that Descartes' famous *Cogito ergo sum* ('I think therefore I am') was meant to exorcise once and for all the demon of doubt raised by Montaigne. In ethics and in religion Pascal had correctly identified the polarities between those who believe that man, by his reason, could achieve virtue, certainty and control of nature and those who rejected such claims and saw relativism, uncertainty and mere conformism as the best man could hope for beyond the pursuit of pleasure. By accepting the half share of truth contained in each extreme, and rejecting the adequacy of either, Pascal broke out of the impasse.

A year later, in January 1656, Pascal was drawn into a controversy at a moment so critical that he had very rapidly to acquire a detailed knowledge of moral theology, a subject which would hardly otherwise have engaged his attention. Equally important to this knowledge was the astonishing flair he showed for satirical writing of exceptional quality, which captured an enthusiastic readership throughout France and abroad. As well as the theological and literary expertise he acquired in the course of writing the eighteen *PLs*, Pascal experienced at first hand the dangers and excitements of clandestine activity on behalf of the cause to which he had so recently committed himself. The anonymity of the *PLs*, only partly dispelled in his lifetime, meant that his services to the truth were never publicly acknowledged, and also, of course, that he escaped prison, or worse punishment. If in one sense his conversion had brought him to a spiritual haven, in another it exposed him (anonymously) to the fiercest blasts of disapproval from the establishment, civil and ecclesiastical, and ensured unremitting hostility from the Jesuits, now represented by more formidable champions than Père Noël.

The first three letters were a last-minute attempt to save Arnauld from being condemned by the Sorbonne. The plight in which Arnauld found himself in January 1656 was irretrievable by ordinary means, that is by technical theological argument, and his supporters turned in desperation to Pascal, who knew the ways of the world so much better than they and might yet rally public opinion. By that time, in view of the forces ranged against Arnauld, nothing could save him from condemnation, but Pascal succeeded brilliantly in bringing the conflict to the attention of men and women who suddenly found that abstract arguments concerning the theology of grace could be made wholly intelligible and even entertaining. They are still so.

Apart from such topical references as those to Arnauld's 'personal' heresy (anything he said automatically became heretical), the two fundamental points at stake were the nature of theological authority and the function of gràce. By confining discussion to professionals (in effect the Sorbonne), theologians had transformed the basic truths of Christianity into forms of words quite divorced from any experiential reality, and Pascal made much of the fact that the Thomists (mostly, but not exclusively, Dominicans) and the Jesuits have ostensibly made common ground against Arnauld by agreeing to use the same words while notoriously meaning two different things by them. Such uneasy tactical alliances might have secured Arnauld's condemnation, but served in the long run only to discredit theology. However technical the arguments and the terms, theology existed only to express intellectually the truths of a faith which is no less accessible to the simple than to the professionals and scholars. There could certainly be no excuse, in Pascal's view, for excluding people intelligent enough to discuss Descartes' philosophy from discussing the faith by which they professed to live. The second point, the function of grace, is the keystone of all Augustinian, including Jansenist, thinking about human nature. It was Pascal's devastating indictment of the consequences of his opponents' theology of grace, illustrated by Jesuit casuistry, which brought home to the widest public the practical implications of what had hitherto seemed a theoretical debate.

As Stoics had shown, it is perfectly possible for men trusting solely in their own resources to lead morally blameless lives, though Pascal regarded their sin of pride as being infinitely reprehensible before God. As portrayed in the *PLs*, the Jesuits permitted, perhaps even encouraged, men to continue morally reprehensible lives on the grounds that they knew how to render such conduct sinless, and this remained Pascal's major charge against them. Put very simply, Pascal's view of Jesuit theology was that it encouraged man to hope for salvation on the cheapest terms possible; in the best case meaning the performance of acts well within man's unaided powers, in the worst case resort to skilful Jesuit advocacy to ensure absolution from the most hideous crimes. This view, not wholly a caricature, must be set against Pascal's own view that all men are so inherently sinful that God's special grace is necessary for men ever to do good; and in order for them to be saved, no amount of advocacy or even moral virtue avails, but solely God's free and unmerited grace. In other words, the Jesuits taught that what Pascal had done in renouncing the world and its values was not required of anyone, and that the most worldly life would never disqualify one of their clients (one can hardly say penitents) from absolution or salvation.

Letters 4–10 inclusive form a masterpiece of polemical journalism, employing the interview technique to make the Jesuits condemn themselves out of their own mouths, in this case through the authorised works on casuistry conveniently anthologised by a Spanish Jesuit, Escobar. Since they cannot deny their own approved texts, they can only accuse Pascal of misrepresentation in principle, and most of Letters 11–18 constitute Pascal's answer to just that charge. Furthermore, their casuistry is only part of a theological system, going beyond moral theology to the theology of grace, which Pascal has no trouble in proving coherent and causally linked.

At first he plays with the co-operative Jesuit interlocutor to find out, in feigned amazement, the general lines of Jesuit teaching, and then he systematically runs through the capital sins examining specific cases (which is, of course, what casuistry is about). He thus builds up a comprehensive picture of the bizarre and wicked conduct for which Jesuit casuists have found some ready excuse. The catalogue is extraordinary, and only reticent on sexual delinquency, about which Pascal deliberately says very little, to avoid charges of prurience and also because of his own natural aversion from such topics. The examples are skilfully chosen so that the reader is left with the impression that thieves and even murderers, let alone gluttons, fornicators and the like, can be painlessly relieved of their guilt if only they enlist a Jesuit confessor. By the tenth Letter, the reader wonders what spiritual reality lies behind a sacrament of supposed penance administered in such a way. Pascal manoeuvres his Jesuit informant into position for the *coup de grâce*. If contrition is not necessary, if none but deliberate, premeditated sin (and not always that) is to be held against the sinner, if no effort or sacrifice is required of the individual, what does it mean to be a Christian or Catholic? The 'good Father' (the words are still proverbial in France) proudly informs his allegedly untutored interviewer that the Jesuits have released man from 'the tiresome duty of loving God'. At this the interview breaks off with an indignant tirade against such blasphemy from the outraged author.

Until this point in the series, the reader of the *PLs* is successively led to believe that the theological condemnation of Arnauld is based on spurious interpretations, that professional theologians are more concerned with terminology than faith, that Jesuits are remarkably, indeed excessively, indulgent to those whose confessions they hear, and that as a result of this laxity man can cheerfully go on serving Mammon. The final revelation that man need not even bother to serve God changes the hitherto fairly genial satire into something quite different, and is an admirable example of how Pascal argues back, as in science, from the phenomenon (the conduct tolerated by the Jesuits) to the root cause (dispensation from the duty to love God). Had he started with the first and greatest commandment, Pascal would have pointed to the saints, known and unknown, throughout the ages and to the blameless life led at Port-Royal by nuns and solitaries. This is, in fact, one of the points he makes in the later Letters, answering specific charges of heresy and impiety concocted by the Jesuits against the Jansenists, though he is at pains to say, truthfully, that he is not one of the Port-Royal community. Faith and morality are inseparable, as he showed, and while he is undoubtedly unfair to the Society of Jesus as a whole, whose roll of honour already included saints and martyrs, he is by no means unfair to the casuists, who were later in the century sternly condemned by Rome. It is relevant, too, that the ingenuity of casuists is essentially an exercise in the use of reason, whereas the sacrament of penance calls for a broken and a contrite heart. It is not before a human judge that the sinner pleads his case, let alone engages someone else to do it for him, and true contrition makes no excuses. Here, then, the Jesuits are confusing the order of reason and that of heart. More seriously they are making a mockery of Christ's sacrifice, as Pascal repeatedly came to write: *ne crux Christi evacuetur*, 'lest the cross of Christ be of no avail', by putting human interest above love of God.

There is a further important reference to the theory of orders in the eighteenth and last Letter, textually recalling Pascal's earlier scientific disagreement with Père Noël. This time he addresses the letter directly to Père Annat, the king's Jesuit confessor, and no longer to his eponymous provincial friend. The point at issue is the legitimacy of Arnauld's condemnation, in view of his enemies' persistent failure to point to the incriminated Five Propositions on which the charge of heresy rested in Jansen's book. Pascal affirms with a sincerity that is beyond question that as a faithful member of the Church he will accept authoritative ruling from Rome that a given proposition is heretical. What he cannot do is accept a ruling that a proposition which neither he nor anyone else can point to is actually contained in a given work, and he once more challenges Annat to justify his claim that the Propositions are textually to be found in Jansen's book. 'How then do we learn the truth about facts? From our eyes, which are the rightful judges of fact, as reason is of natural and intelligible things, and faith of things supernatural and revealed'.

The last few Letters, much more serious in tone than the others, come closer to apologetic writing than to satire, and show once again the persistence of certain habits of thought, originally acquired in scientific inquiry, in the new field of religion. The theory of orders remains paramount, but both in the conversation with Saci and in the *PLs* the practical, daily consequences of Pascal's conversion to Christ are assimilated to the earlier pattern. There can be no doubt that the reason for Pascal's continued popularity among so many and diverse readers lies in his exceptional ability to make real and concrete some of the deepest preoccupations of humanity. His invariable criterion in science, technology, religion or any other subject was 'does the theory work in practice?' When faced with the mysteries of faith, above and beyond rational demonstration, he always depicted them in terms of what answers they gave to practical problems and what practical consequences followed once an individual assented to them.

The *Conversation with M. de Saci* was not published until long after Pascal's death, and the *PLs* were not publicly acknowledged. Nevertheless, enough was known of Port-Royal's distinguished friend for him to receive a number of requests to draft documents on the current controversy, especially from clergy in Paris, who were concerned about the Signature (to the formulary condemning the *Augustinus* without qualification). The clarity and force of these pamphlets is still evident, but their interest is historical. Thus obliged to learn a lot about theology in a short time, Pascal composed some brief essays on grace, the first of which was a model of exposition. He gave clear and succinct statements of the teaching of the principal theological factions in dispute, the Molinists, the Calvinists and finally the Augustinians, the party to which he and the Jansenists belonged. It is not immediately apparent to the layman just what practical consequences the different doctrines on grace, free will and predestination have for the ordinary believer, but in his final summary Pascal makes it clear:

All men are obliged to believe . . . that they belong to this small number of the elect whom Jesus Christ wishes to save, and never to judge of any of the men living on earth, however wicked and impious they may be, as long as a single moment of life remains, that they are not numbered among the predestined, leaving discernment of the elect and the damned as an impenetrable secret of God, which obliges them to do for such men whatever may contribute to their salvation.

Not a word is wasted, and the last phrase in particular leaves the Christian no choice but to love his neighbour effectively. Neither the railing denunciations of the extreme Calvinist nor the bland assurance of the worldly Jesuit are compatible with this balanced statement of a Christian's inescapable duty to God, to himself and to others. From what is known of his life after his conversion, it seems that Pascal did his best to live up to his own prescription.

In a very different context, some advice given to a young nobleman comes to a similar conclusion. In a text actually written by Pierre Nicole, Arnauld's closest associate, but apparently reproducing with high fidelity three brief essays by Pascal of about 1660 (*On the Noble Estate*), we find Pascal advising a young man, probably the duc de Chevreuse, twenty-year-old son of the fervent Jansenist duc de Luynes, on the implications of his rank. Pascal stresses at the beginning that the privileges inherited from ancestors, aristocratic or even royal, rest on no natural right but on purely human decree, as arbitrary in its application as all other human decrees, and equally subject to reversal. God, however, allows society to legislate, and it thus becomes unjust to break any established law, but no less unjust than to assume that the possession of privilege arises from or is due to personal merit.

The second essay distinguishes between conventional greatness (*grandeurs d'établissement*), such as titles of nobility, and natural greatness, such as intellectual, physical or moral eminence. Proper respect is due to each, but a dishonourable duke would be entitled to external marks of respect even if accompanied by inward contempt. Here again the idea of orders is clearly apparent.

The last essay brings this out with the greatest clarity. The young man is told that the true estate of the noble is to be 'master of numerous objects of human concupiscence and thus able to satisfy the needs and desires of many'. God, on the other hand, is 'properly speaking the king of charity', because the devout ask of him the gifts of charity, just as the noble is the 'king of concupiscence'. The familiar Augustinan, and Pauline, picture of the two kingdoms leads on to a final paradox. The noble should do all within his power to satisfy the material needs of those dependent on him, but he should not exercise his power with brutal domination. By such humane behaviour in the material order he will at least be properly exercising his kingship, but if he stops at that he will be lost. 'At least you will be doing so as an *honnête homme*', unlike others guilty of such dishonourable sins as violence and blasphemy, but 'it is indeed always very foolish to bring about one's own damnation; and that is why you should not stop at that', that is, material largesse. 'You must despise concupiscence and its kingdom, and aspire to the kingdom of charity, in which all the subjects breathe nothing but charity and desire only the gifts of charity.' In other words, the material world has perfectly legitimate values which the responsible man will respect as such, but no amount of material beneficence can have the slightest value as a work of charity unless prompted by charitable motives, and not purely human ones.

These brief essays underline once more Pascal's insistence on the concurrent but totally separate existence of two worlds, that of charity on the one hand, where God alone is king, and of concupiscence, or worldly values, on the other, in which the materially (or even the intellectually) powerful have their rule, although one which will lead them to damnation unless they are redeemed by charity.

Pascal was neither a sociologist nor a political philosopher. To him the most pressing human problems were spiritual ones, capable only of a spiritual solution, or short-term practical ones, like the relief of a neighbour's poverty. To proffer a political remedy for the human condition was, he thought, as futile as to attempt to prescribe laws for the inhabitants of a madhouse. Nevertheless, Pascal had his political preferences, and as well as the advice given to the young noble, he offered in the *PLs* and in the first part of the *Pensées* some penetrating, though characteristically pessimistic, insights into the workings of human society.

Many of Pascal's views, and examples, derive from Montaigne. Thus he held that there was no absolute political justice. Standards varied from one country to another; and local custom was the only source of political authority. There was nothing intrinsically good about prevailing political arrangements. Hereditary monarchs and aristocrats were, as we have just seen, in no way personally superior to other men. Private property was a usurpation and war absurd. Nevertheless, political institutions of some kind were necessary to prevent the social disintegration which would be produced by allowing men to gratify their selfish impulses unrestrained. For Pascal the highest political priority was peace and strong government; and it did not matter what form that government took as long as it was effective. The wise citizen would not seek political participation, but would live simply and quietly, away from the political arena.

Pascal thus aligned himself with the long Christian tradition, dating from St Augustine, according to which the State was an artificial contrivance, brought into being by the fact of human sin. He totally rejected the alternative tradition, stemming from Aristotle, who had represented the State as a natural growth, offering maximum scope for human fulfilment.

Yet though the State for Pascal was essentially a repressive force, keeping the anarchic tendencies of human nature at bay, it did not maintain its authority by force alone. It is true that all kings were ultimately reliant on military strength. But their judges and other subordinate officers would sustain their position by wearing distinctive dress, using special ceremonies and creating imaginary bonds of respect. Indeed he applied the same principle to doctors, professors and preachers, among others, who would soon forfeit respect if dressed like ordinary men. It is in his recognition of the element of theatricality and illusion (what he called 'imagination') involved in the workings of social hierarchy that Pascal shows himself at his sociologically most acute.

Pascal's treatment of all the topics discussed in this chapter lead him to the same conclusion: human beings left to their own resources, unaided by God, could only come to grief. What he regarded as the false philosophy of Montaigne and Epictetus concealed from man the full truth of his dual nature, thus inculcating either arrogance or indifference. The false theology of the Jesuits and their allies castigated in the *PLs* led them to condone immoral and even criminal conduct and was, in Pascal's view, nowhere more reprehensible than when it absolved man from the duty of loving God. The false values of social and political life derived both from the abuse of power and from acquiescence in conventions which honoured a façade while ignoring the emptiness it concealed. Such a profoundly gloomy picture of man's corruption without God, combined with the literary experience gained from writing the phenomenally successful *PLs*, formed the prelude and preparation for Pascal's greatest work, the *Pensées*. There he was to elaborate and focus the themes treated in his earlier writings, together with the very varied experience, social, scientific and spiritual, of his life up to then.

4 Origin and plan of the *Pensées*

It is not known who or what specially impelled Pascal to embark
upon his *Apology for the Christian Religion*, which survives only
in the incomplete form of the *Pensées*, but such a project seems
a logical enough consequence of his own conversion, and of the
views summarised in the discussions with Saci and of the *PLs*.
The mainly negative, but by no means sterile, effect of the latter
may well have been the initial cause of Pascal's decision to follow
polemic with apologetic. The work seems first to have taken
definite shape in 1658, and was halted by his death four years
later.

Recent and continuing scholarship has brought us closer to
Pascal's successive intentions than seemed possible forty years
ago. It has above all enabled a wide measure of agreement on the
objective criteria governing edition of the *Pensées*, so that the
almost entirely subjective editorial arrangements invariably
offered from Pascal's death up to the Tourneur edition of 1938
or even that of Lafuma in 1951 remain only as evidence that
tradition counts for more than accuracy in the eyes of some
publishers. The discovery which permitted objectivity to take
over was made when a table of contents, long known but largely
ignored, was conclusively proved in 1953 to be a direct copy of a
table actually written in Pascal's hand and since lost. Henceforth,
twenty-eight chapters with specific titles, specific contents and a
specific order have been universally accepted as corresponding
with Pascal's last recorded intentions, which is very far from
saying that the final work would have had either twenty-eight
chapters or those particular titles. Disagreement and uncertainty
over detail persists, and in some cases – notably the internal order
within chapters – will probably never be resolved, but the modern
reader can be confident of finding editions that scrupulously
respect Pascal's order, present a text with fewer misreadings than
ever before and enable him to form some idea of what the completed work might have looked like.

The intricacies of the textual problem are endless, but in very simple terms Pascal's method of composition was as follows. He used large sheets of paper, and when he was making notes separated each entry on a given sheet by a horizontal stroke, sometimes, of course, filling up the whole sheet with a continuous entry. His method of classification, or filing system, was quite common in his day: he would cut the large sheets into as many strips as there were entries, and thread these strips together, passing a string through a hole in the corner of each, to form a bundle, corresponding to a chapter heading in the table of contents. The fragments thus classified in twenty-eight bundles (*liasses*) make up about one third of a modern edition. In addition, he left other papers, varying in length from simple sentences to several continuous pages, and arranged them in thirty-five identifiable units, not threaded or given chapter headings, to make up something like half the total; some, however, belong not to the *Apology* but to other, usually identifiable, works. The original manuscript of most of these fragments survives, and early in the eighteenth century they were pasted into an album, later bound, in an order which, without being wholly random, is largely dictated by purely physical considerations (fragments were trimmed to fit a sheet).

The basis of all serious modern editions is the two copies made of the original soon after Pascal's death, which both maintain the same order of the twenty-eight chapters as well as the internal order of the thirty-five other units, but differ significantly in the relative arrangement of the latter between themselves. Finally there are various papers, original or reliable copies from various sources, mostly not intended for the *Apology,* but of considerable interest, which make up the last sixth or so of the modern edition. It is amazing, and almost without parallel, that we should possess the original manuscript of a seventeenth-century work, with all the erasures, additions and changes which permit us to reconstruct much of Pascal's thought, and check all doubtful readings. The original and both copies can be seen at the Bibliothèque Nationale in Paris.

From this it should be clear that the *Pensées* as we know them are far from being equivalent to the projected *Apology*, but rather afford a view of successive stages in Pascal's composition and, in the physical form in which the text survives, bear witness to the often quite different interests he was concurrently pursuing.

The latest research suggests, with a high degree of probability, that Pascal first contemplated a treatise on miracles, arising from that of the Holy Thorn in 1657 (the relic which, it was claimed, had cured his niece of a fistula in the eye). Three papers (Series XXXII–XXXIV) belong to that project. He then, or possibly earlier, began an examination of the credentials of the Pentateuch, based on Esdras. The relevant papers survive in the Second Copy (Series XXXV). Miracles and exegesis continued to interest him, but the next stage, that of the twenty-eight chapters, was in every way more comprehensive in content and more elaborate in structure.

Any apology for Christianity must have some audience in mind, whether of identifiable views or not, because the arguments required to convince an African peasant will obviously be different from those addressed to an educated Chinese. What Pascal planned was no handbook for missionaries in far-off lands, nor yet a brief for a Christian advocate in a debate with professional theologians of other faiths. He was aiming specifically, and at times by name, at members of the social world from which his conversion had removed him. These were the cultured, intelligent *libertins* (free-thinkers) who preferred polite agnosticism to militant atheism, whose ideal was *honnêteté*, a gentlemanly code governed more by etiquette than ethics, and whose model was Montaigne, generally regarded in the seventeenth century as the arch-sceptic and *honnête homme*. Some of these people were attracted by rationalism, by Descartes or the Stoics, but most of them led lives devoted as far as possible to the pursuit of pleasure and the gratification of their egos. Many of the case histories satirised in the *PLs*, ranging from duels to debauchery, are typical of this class, and total lack of faith did not necessarily deter them from going through the motions of religious practice for social, or even prudential, reasons. The comedies of Molière, the memoirs of Retz, the sermons of Bossuet, the *Maxims* of La

Rochefoucauld depict the refined manners and moral emptiness of the people whom Pascal sought to convert.

The *Apology* would have meant little to the peasants and artisans for whom religion was perhaps the only comfort in a life of poverty and toil. It spoke for the more educated but still modest Catholics of town and country who took seriously their Christian duty of charity to their neighbour and accepted the frugal way of life they had inherited. It spoke, too, for those, like Pascal, of independent means, who had sacrificed luxury for sufficiency out of genuine Christian conviction. Those to whom it was directed were the easy-going, heedless materialists for whom tomorrow was another day and self-interest the best investment. It is precisely because economic development has brought such standards within reach, or at least sight, of all in the Western world today that a book originally written for a numerically tiny minority is now so popular.

The traditional proofs of the existence of God had been from the effects demonstrable in the natural world back to the first cause. From the form of deism thus proved, the passage across to Christian revelation was usually constructed from an appeal to faith in divine goodness and omnipotence. When Descartes set out to found his science on metaphysics, his proof of the existence of God, first seen in the *Discours*, then, in 1640, in the much more detailed *Meditations,* relied not on the external world of nature but solely on his own existence as a thinking being. Whatever the validity of Descartes' proofs (and they were disputed in his own day), it is abundantly clear that no possible rational way lay open to effect the transition from this new version of deism to Christian revelation. Pascal indeed says that such deism is almost as far from Christianity as outright atheism (449).

For his *Apology*, Pascal explicitly rejected proofs from effects in the natural order (3); he also, and more importantly, rejected proofs by reason alone. Taking a leaf from Descartes' book, no less than from Montaigne's, Pascal insisted that man must begin with self-knowledge. There the resemblance stopped. Montaigne had admitted that presumption was man's natural malady, but had thought to cure it with massive doses of scepticism, followed by a prolonged course of empiricism. Descartes was highly delighted with the rational image reflected in his own mirror. Pascal, on the other hand, saw man's natural state as sick, in Augustinian terms irremediably corrupt, but in secular language simply wretched. It is on this wretchedness that Pascal concentrates as the first demonstrable effect to be linked with an as yet unknown cause. The wretchedness does not, however, constitute the whole of the human condition, for it is inseparably, though mysteriously, associated with a greatness in man, of which, despite all his corruption, traces subsist. This dualism inherent in human nature provides the starting point and framework for the *Apology*. The opening chapter of the *Pensées*, headed 'Order', leaves no room for doubt:

First part: Wretchedness of man without God.
Second part: Happiness of man with God.
otherwise
First part: Nature is corrupt, proved by nature itself.
Second part: There is a Redeemer, proved by Scripture. (6)

From the very first Pascal planned to go straight from the facts of the human condition to the truth of the Redemption, without bringing in deism at any stage.

The pattern already seen in the discussion with M. de Saci is here repeated in a slightly different form. In each case two contradictory truths about man are presented, in each case the contradiction can only be reconciled by admitting a third truth, containing and superseding the other two. This dialectic runs right through the *Pensées*, and would have been equally evident in the *Apology* had it ever been completed, but, it must be repeated, has nothing to do with the now familiar dialectic of thesis, antithesis, synthesis. In the order of exposition, Christianity comes last, but in the order of truth and reality it always comes first.

This same introductory chapter 'Order' gives valuable indications of the actual form the finished *Apology* would have taken. There is one reference to 'order by dialogues' (2) and five to 'letters' (4, 5, 7, 9, 11). A moment's thought will show that these need not be alternative or mutually exclusive solutions, because the first ten *PLs* had contained within an epistolary framework some of the most spirited dialogues ever written in French, but examination of the text of the *Pensées* makes it virtually certain that both dialogue and letter would have been employed. The essential difference is that in dialogue the interlocutor speaks for himself, whilst in a letter his words, if quoted, are always at one remove from immediate exchange. The two things that seem reasonably certain are that the *Apology* would not have been a treatise, and that it would not have preserved the fragmentary form which makes so many detached phrases read like independent aphorisms.

Two consequences seem to follow from these formal considerations: the *ad hominem* element clearly visible in the *Pensées* would have been continuously stressed in the *Apology*, so that the *libertin* interlocutor would eventually have been characterised as individually as 'the good Father' of the *PLs*, and, secondly, as the argument progressed, his questions and reactions would show the successive stages of his nascent faith. Pascal was transmitting not fixed and abstract theological dogma, but a living faith and specific way of life, and though the very detailed exegesis of the Old and New Testaments contained in the *Pensées* does not, as it stands, suggest a very personal approach, the concluding chapter on 'Christian Morality' clearly does, and is the purpose of the whole exercise. The *honnête homme* may well, like the Stoic, lead a morally commendable life without professing any but a secular ethic, whilst the professing Christian may well fail to match his deeds to his words. But the religion for which Pascal is undertaking an apology demands both faith and works, claiming that one will follow from the other.

Besides these formal considerations of form and intention, one of methodology must be added. In rejecting such rationalist claims as those of Descartes, Pascal was manifestly not rejecting reason itself so much as its misuse. A reasoned apology must appeal to and satisfy the reason, and Pascal constantly affirms his intention to do just that. However, as with the dialectic of contradictions, he never stops at a single stage of a multiple argument, and the *Pensées* exemplify the fullest and final version of his theory of orders. Here, for perhaps the first time, the three orders are presented not merely as separate entities, enjoying autonomy in their own realms, but very frequently in a hierarchy of excellence. The crucial apologetic arguments depend on this treatment of orders. In particular, the substantial part of the argument involving the 'hidden God' can only be understood in the light of this new version of the orders.

The dualism of body and mind (or spirit) was the basis of Cartesianism, and, with different emphasis, of Platonism and its Christian mystical derivatives. In both cases the body is presented as the animal, inferior, even hostile, part of man, subject to passions and sensory illusions, like colour blindness, which hamper the operation of man's higher nature, and is condemned to corruption at death. Montaigne had, perhaps perversely, stressed man's physical, and thus fallible, nature in his attack on reason, and in more general terms recognised that the body plays a large part in forming personality. Pascal had already in his earliest work allotted a vital role to the senses in experimental method, checking rational hypotheses and providing concrete evidence to balance abstract reasoning, but in the *Pensées* a whole new range of functions and associations is attached to the body. In the first few fragments there are two important references to 'the Machine' and a very late fragment begins:

For we must make no mistake about ourselves: we are as much automaton as mind ... Proofs only convince the mind; habit provides the strongest proofs and those that are most believed. It inclines the automaton, which leads the mind unconsciously along with it. (821)

This ties in exactly with the concluding advice in the Wager fragment (418): when the sceptic has been intellectually convinced that opting for God's existence is in accordance with the rational laws of probability, he asks what he should do next. He is told: 'learn from those who were once bound like you and who now wager all they have ... They behaved just as if they did believe, taking holy water, having masses said, and so on. That will make you believe quite naturally, and will make you more docile.' The last word is *abêtira* in French, meaning to reduce to the status of unthinking animals, for whom the description *bête-machine* was a commonplace in seventeenth-century thought.

Since it is reason that asks questions and encourages arrogance (Montaigne had linked curiosity and presumption together as man's natural maladies), Pascal's respect for the unthinking, automatic nature of man, for conditioned reflexes, is of the highest importance in his apology. At the same time, his treatment of body is affected by his understanding of Pauline and biblical tradition in general, so that, for example, 'carnal' and 'flesh' become unequivocally pejorative. Consequently the range of associations now applying to the order of body is much wider than previously.

With reason or mind (*esprit*) there is less room for complications, but even so the range is considerable. As well as all the obvious usages referring to intellectual operations, there are two value judgements of crucial importance. Constantly, and especially in such fragments as the Wager, Pascal stresses the limits and inadequacy of intellect faced with a whole series of problems. He explicitly denies, for instance, that we can know first principles by reason (thereby contradicting Descartes), and maintains that 'Principles are felt, propositions proved, and both with certainty though by different means' (110). At the other end of the scale, in the Wager, he claims that the existence of God, and our own ultimate destination, is beyond proof, whence his resort to a wager: 'Reason cannot make you choose either, reason cannot prove either wrong.' (That is, God's existence or non-existence: 418.)

But if such statements confine reason within boundaries squeezed on either side by other faculties or orders, Pascal leaves no doubt as to the true value of reason. One of his most celebrated fragments puts it succinctly: 'Man is only a reed, the weakest in nature, but he is a thinking reed ... Thus all our dignity consists in thought' (200).

The third order is the most important and the most controversial. In previous formulations he had spoken of faith, in the context of different kinds of authority, but in the *Pensées* the same, or a similar, kind of opposition to body and mind is conveyed by words not used in his earlier works, especially 'heart' and 'charity'. There can be little doubt that he is thinking of the same order when he speaks of heart providing the first principles which reason cannot supply (110 above), of habit inculcating belief, 'Incline my heart' (821) and above all:

The heart has its order, the mind has its own, which uses principles and demonstrations . . . Jesus Christ and St Paul possess the order of charity, not of the mind, for they wished to humble, not to teach . . . This order consists mainly in digressions upon each point which relates to the end, so that this shall be kept always in sight. (298)

In this last fragment 'heart' and 'charity' are used interchangeably, and provided with a specific methodology, in opposition to that of mind. The other fundamental antithesis sets 'charity' against 'concupiscence' and lies behind the many examples of typology (*figures*). Heart can be turned upwards, to charity and things of the spirit (Christ as saviour), or downwards, to concupiscence and things of the flesh (Christ as earthly king), and according to its disposition will affect, one might almost say ground, the operations of mind, itself corrupt by nature but capable of being turned to right use if moved by grace.

Thus the *Apology* aimed at integrating the three orders, each used as it was meant to be used, but in a clear hierarchy of excellence since the end in sight was God. Fragmentary as they are, the *Pensées* preserve this plan of showing faith to be the result of God inclining our hearts, rather than convincing our minds, and doing so solely and always through Christ, without whom it is not possible to know God at all.

5 Man without God

Although Pascal never conceived of his *Apology* as a linear argument, and indeed explicitly stated the necessity for a series of convergent approaches to the whole problem of man and God, there is a first premiss without which the rest collapses. His critics up to the present day have always attacked this premiss, without necessarily rejecting his conclusion, and it is a fair assumption that the exact opposite is true of the majority of his readers. The categorical statement that man is wretched constitutes the basis of Pascal's entire argument, and while definitions of wretchedness are open to discussion, the thesis as such is not if the argument is to proceed. That many people much of the time are discontented with life is very probable; that such discontent is an essential feature of the human condition, arising from natural wretchedness, is a claim vehemently opposed for a whole variety of reasons even by those who are most discontented. The right to happiness is obscurely felt to be part of the human lot; the search, however vain, is unremitting. Even of those who feel that they are happy, few fail to recognise that loss of health, prosperity or loved ones could instantly plunge them into misery. If security and fulfilment would be generally accepted as components of happiness, insecurity and frustration clearly belong to what Pascal would call wretchedness. The point at issue is which of the two states, happiness or wretchedness, is, in any sense, natural to man.

The question of what constitutes human nature had been given a new twist by Montaigne, who for polemical reasons had contrasted the virtues of primitive tribes in America with the vices of those coming from Europe supposedly to civilise them. The cult of the noble savage, like that of the golden age or the pastoral idyll, was vaguely nostalgic, a picturesque idealism rather than a serious philosophy. The desire to make a fresh start, individually or collectively, expressed dissatisfaction with the existing state of affairs rather than positive desire for a return to cruder things. In any case, even the professedly anti-intellectual Montaigne gave the game away when, like every other humanist, he chose as his ideal man Socrates and not some feathered brave from Brazil. In so doing he acknowledged that the right use of reason leads to greater moral excellence than mere obedience to instinct, even if the wrong use of reason led to a worse than bestial depravity. For all the polemic, Montaigne did not deny that human nature is essentially rational as well as instinctive and physical, like the animals, but for him rational meant fallible, as the *Essays* constantly show. Much of the book is devoted to a comprehensive catalogue of behaviour, values, laws, institutions in different countries and different times, designed to prove that all is relative, there is no natural law or natural morality, and reason, being fallible, is no better a criterion than mere whim.

Pascal begins, like Montaigne and Socrates before him, with the demand that man should know himself. Man's condition is 'inconstancy, boredom, anxiety' (24) and much of the time he is led by the nose by the 'deceptive powers' of imagination, vanity and so on masquerading as reality. The dualism of his nature is clearly stated: 'Instinct and reason, signs of two natures' (112). Immediately afterwards comes a fragment with the title 'thinking reed', fully explained only later: 'Man is only a reed, the weakest in nature, but he is a thinking reed.' (200) Then a series of fragments points out that what in animals and trees, for example, is merely their natural state, in man becomes wretchedness because of his awareness through reason. This self-awareness is at once the reminder of wretchedness and the proof of greatness lost, 'the wretchedness of a dispossessed king' (116). An earlier quotation from Ecclesiastes goes some way to explaining what Pascal means by wretchedness: 'Anyone is unhappy who wills but cannot do. Now he wants to be happy and assured of some truth, and yet he is equally incapable of knowing and not desiring to know. He cannot even doubt' (75). Elsewhere he adds the physical dimension, showing man, like all other creatures, subject to disease, death and destruction, but unable to do anything about it, while striving incessantly against the inevitable.

In this line of argument Pascal follows Montaigne, and refers extensively to examples and phrases of the *Essays*. But since his purpose is quite different, he goes further in his analysis and looks for the why as well as the how of such a paradoxical situation as that of man. Once Montaigne had demolished the pretensions of reason, he was content to live his life as it came, but in the *Conversation with M. de Saci* Pascal had signified his total disagreement with such a course. Pride must, of course, be put down, but there remained the problem of inertia which, by muffling wretchedness, deadened, too, any regret for greatness lost, let alone the hope of regaining it. Pascal's reaction to Montaigne's flight to a hammock of ignorance and indolence is to rock it so vigorously that even the bare ground of wretchedness below seems preferable. He uses every device of style to instil in his reader a feeling of desperate insecurity. At the same time, he never ceases to insist that a remedy is available if man will only seek it outside himself and his feeble reason: 'Man transcends man' (131). If man remains within the natural order, whether of instinct, or reason, or both, he will never get beyond his wretchedness.

A long fragment at the end of the section 'Contradictions' introduces another aspect of man's dualism, impervious to dogmatism and scepticism alike. Nature (or instinct) rejects scepticism, reason rejects dogmatism: how, then, is man to resolve the hopeless paradox of his own nature? How can he take the first step towards wisdom and know himself? Pascal interrupts a remorseless string of perplexing questions to give the simple answer 'Listen to God.' Without some antecedent corruption, man would enjoy the truth and happiness he now vainly seeks, but had he never known such truth and happiness he would not think to seek it. Once again 'man infinitely transcends man, and without the aid of faith he would remain incomprehensible to himself'. The key to the riddle is original sin, the dualism thus revealed is that of grace and corruption, corresponding to greatness and wretchedness. The Fall, wholly inaccessible to reason or instinct, cuts through the knot: man is neither animal nor divine, but both, divine through grace, animal through corruption.

The similarity of this fragment (131) to the *Conversation with M. de Saci* is inevitable, given that they both treat the theme of scepticism versus dogmatism, Montaigne versus Epictetus. In the

Pensées both problem and solution are posed in more radical terms, involving the whole of human chronology, and forming part of a much wider argument, in which Christ and the Gospel have yet to appear. Significantly, the next section is devoted to man's instinctive response to such an unpalatable truth about himself, and contains one long and several shorter fragments on diversion. The first goes straight back to the theme of wretchedness: 'If man were happy, the less he were diverted the happier he would be' (132). Pascal adds that the happiness gained from diversion is illusory, since it depends on something outside, merely distracting us momentarily from the painful truth: 'the sole cause of man's unhappiness is that he does not know how to stay quietly in his room' (136), because if he did he would become bored, thought would supervene and realisation of his wretchedness would become so unbearable that new diversion would have to be sought. The examples of diversion enumerated by Pascal are of course those common to the leisured classes of his own day, and by no means synonymous with amusement: for example, military service, gambling, hunting, billiards and mathematical problems. It must be remembered that whatever the spread of his readership today, he was in fact addressing his argument strictly *ad hominem* to representatives of a numerically very small élite.

So far Pascal has concentrated on the problem, and has shown only a small part of the solution. Man is a paradoxical creature, split into two parts variously described as wretchedness and greatness, instinct and reason; the origin of his fruitless search for happiness lies in the past history of mankind, and not in that of the individual; all human values and justice are relative, human life provisional and diversions futile. The only positive pointer is that we should listen to God and recognise that our present state represents a fall from our true and original nature, which was grace. Thus the ubiquitous theory of orders once more provides the pattern: the purely human dualism of mind and matter must be transcended, which can only be done by grace, a third order not within our control, but which comes as a free, unearned gift from God. So long as we fail to admit that man must transcend man, Pascal says, we shall be locked in the prison of human limitations. Worse than that, the natural selfishness of each man left to himself means that this is solitary confinement. The collective price imposed on all mankind for the fall (as yet unspecified) into corruption has to be paid by each of us individually until the end of time, unless we use the gift of thought for the submissiveness that brings release instead of for the arrogance that puts us behind bars. Even those philosophers who preach and practise brotherly love and human solidarity are still hemmed in by man's radical inability to change his human condition, and are pinning such faith as they have on a species as fallible collectively as they themselves are individually.

The rest of the *Pensées* reiterates the three themes just mentioned: the theory of orders (with a supernatural order added to the natural orders of body and mind), the emphasis on a historical perspective (beginning with Adam and the Fall) and the crippling moral effects of selfishness, whether active self-seeking or mere inertia. Thus the contention that man is wretched is from the first attached to the proviso 'without God' and the proofs of the wretchedness are drawn from observation of man's situation under a variety of headings – cosmic, social, private. A striking feature of Pascal's thought and style is the obsessive, haunting variation on the same small number of basic themes and patterns.

The long fragment entitled *APR* (149: almost certainly *A Port-Royal*, referring to an occasion on which he gave a summary of his *Apology* as then conceived to his friends at Port-Royal) draws these themes together and shows that one of Pascal's principal arguments is achieved by process of elimination. He sets out the broad diagnosis of man's ills, says that the true religion will be that which most adequately deals with them and reviews other religions and philosophies to see whether they compare in efficacy with Christianity. He lets the wisdom of God speak in person, defining very exactly what took place at the Fall:

I created man holy, innocent, perfect . . . Man's eye then beheld the majesty of God . . . But he could not bear such great glory without falling into presumption. He wanted to make himself his own centre and do without my help. He withdrew from my rule, setting himself up as my equal in his desire to find happiness in himself . . .

The argument goes on to show that the only alternatives then left open to man derived from his dual nature: 'the pride that withdraws you from God, the concupiscence that binds you to the earth', that is, indulgence of intellectual and physical natures respectively. Then, and only then, does Pascal introduce the specifically and uniquely Christian stage of his argument: 'God's will has been to redeem men and open the way of salvation to those who seek it.' The fragment breaks off shortly afterwards, without amplifying the Christian message.

Most of the arguments that follow are no longer concerned with man's wretchedness but with the compelling necessity to do something about it. The theme of death begins to become insistent: 'It is absurd of us to rely on the company of our fellows, as wretched and helpless as we are; they will not help us; we shall die alone' (151); 'It affects our whole life to know whether the soul is mortal or immortal' (164); and the striking: 'the last act is bloody, however fine the rest of the play. They throw earth over your head and it is finished for ever' (165). The enigma of this life was upsetting enough, but with the question mark of the hereafter Pascal introduces the idea of the abyss confronting man. In the section headed 'Transition from knowledge of Man to knowledge of God', the theme of vertigo induced by the abyss finds its finest and most sustained expression in the fragment called 'Disproportion of Man' (199).

These six pages put man in a cosmic perspective between the infinitely great, revealed by the telescope, and the infinitely small, revealed by the microscope (a recent novelty), and have gained rather than lost in actuality with the progress of science over the past three centuries. An isolated fragment incorporated in slightly different form in the fuller draft sums up Pascal's message: 'The eternal silence of these infinite spaces fills me with dread' (201), though the fuller context (198) makes it clear that such dread assails only those dependent on their own resources. Man occupies a middle station between the two extremes so insignificant that differences between individual human specks in space are meaningless.

The immediately succeeding fragment is that which explains the earlier cryptic mention of the 'thinking reed' and combines it with the theme of death to marked effect: 'But even if the universe were to crush him, man would still be nobler than his slayer, because he knows that he is dying and the advantage the universe has over him. The universe knows nothing of this. Thus all our dignity consists in thought' (200). No longer sovereign reason, 'master and possessor of nature', but reason as humble self-awareness marks man out from the vastness of the cosmos above and the tininess of the miniature world below him.

Here at the mid-point (chapter 14 out of 28), the analysis of man's state gives way to a discussion of the remedies proposed by other religions, and, finally, by Christianity. It is man's special relationship to a God he has lost that occupies most of this first part, not, as we see now, a created, and, in that sense, natural wretchedness, but a second nature brought upon man by his own presumption and folly. It is Pascal's case that Christianity alone makes sense of man's predicament, reconciles the greatness and the wretchedness and gives fallen man a lifeline back to grace, and that no other remedy offered, secular or religious, comes anywhere near a solution. Here, as always, the formulation of the problem presupposes the shape of the solution. What distinguishes Pascal's treatment of a well-worn theme is the extraordinarily comprehensive presentation of man in such a range of contexts and activities, and, evidently, a style of quite peculiar intensity and vigour, combining poetry and logic, vision and the common touch.

The texts so far discussed all come from the classified papers, because these reflect an internal order of which one can be reasonably sure. Elaborations of the same arguments occur, however, some at greater length among the papers not so filed, and add substantially to what has already been said. One such important, though brief, elaboration comes in a fragment addressed by name to the gambler Daniel Mitton, generally recognised as the prototype of the worldly unbeliever for whom the *Apology* was specifically intended.

The self is hateful. You cover it up, Mitton, but that does not mean that you take it away. So you are still hateful . . . In a word the self has two characteristics. It is unjust in itself for making itself centre of everything: it is a nuisance to others in that it tries to subjugate them, for each self is the enemy of all the others and would like to tyrannise them. (597)

It is remarkable how the theme of man at the centre, first instead of God, then between the two infinites of great and small and now in society, recurs in such varied contexts but always pointing out the same defect.

Another celebrated fragment that takes up an earlier theme is that of the so-called Wager (418: properly 'infinity-nothing'). It has seized the imagination of innumerable readers, puzzled or exasperated those for whom the mathematical argument is either too recondite or technically dubious, and it remains indispensable for understanding Pascal's attitude to an *Apology* designed to convert. From the march and content of the argument, the passage is most probably intended to come at the hinge of the *Apology*, at the point when the unbeliever is ready to give Christianity a trial.

Pascal begins with the fact that we accept the existence of mathematical infinity, though our minds can never know it, and proceeds to show that though rational proof cannot establish the existence of God, it is against reason to withhold our judgement on this, the most important question in our lives. We must wager, as he puts it, on whether the coin will come down heads or tails. His interlocutor at once objects: 'The right thing is not to wager at all', to which Pascal replies: 'Yes, but you must wager. There is no choice, you are already committed.' These last words (in French *vous êtes déjà embarqué*) may be denounced as emotional blackmail, but the plain fact is that refusal to wager, or at least to seek, is, as Pascal says, a choice entailing precisely the same consequences as negative choice. Nor is it enough to represent such agnosticism as a device for buying time because, in Pascal's terms, time (our life span) is an integral part of the stake.

The complex mathematical details need not be examined here, but Pascal's conclusion sums them up in simple language: one should wager for the existence of God on grounds of pure self-interest 'when the stakes are finite [our earthly lives] in a game where there are even chances of winning and losing and an infinite prize [eternal life] to be won'. The ensuing dialogue is more important than the mathematics:

I am being forced to wager, and I am not free; I am being held fast and I am so made that I cannot believe. What do you want me to do then? — That is true, but at least get it into your head that if you are unable to believe it is because of your passions, since reason impels you to believe and yet you cannot do so.

The remedy for this resistance is to subdue the passions by habit, by going through the external motions of faith (for example, taking holy water, having masses said), which will enable the unthinking reflex to replace self-will, in Pascal's words *cela vous abêtira*, 'That will make you more docile, more like a trained animal'.

Once again, the dualism in man is stressed, this time reason and passions, will and habit, and only when reason has submitted and the passions have been subdued can grace take over. The concluding passage, headed 'End of this address', surely goes further to explain the enduring success of the *Pensées* than the earlier display of mathematical subtlety:

Now what harm will come to you from choosing this course? You will be faithful, honest, humble, grateful, full of good works, a sincere, true friend ... If my words please you and seem cogent, you must know that they come from a man who went down upon his knees before and after to pray this infinite and indivisible being, to whom he submits his own, that he might bring your being also to submit to him for your own good and for his glory.

Several other passages, some very long, express Pascal's indignation at those who refuse to seek and scoff at those who do, but none sums up the predicament of man's wretchedness without God with such brutal force as this isolated fragment:

Imagine a number of men in chains, all under sentence of death, some of whom are each day butchered in the sight of the others; those remaining see their own condition in that of their fellows, and looking at each other with grief and despair await their turn. This is an image of the human condition. (434)

The patently emotive ring of such a passage is justified by Pascal's view that the passions are an obstacle to faith even when reason is not. It is the whole man who must be saved, so that body, mind and heart strive together for the same goal. The alternative is a life built on shifting sand, followed by the certainty of a death leading to an unknown abyss more terrifying than the vastness of space in which we precariously pass our lives. Thought alone, not heedless diversion, can point the way to safety.

6 Man with God

The picture of man's wretchedness described by Pascal is inseparable from the idea of a happiness no longer enjoyed. The condemnation of human weakness and vanity could properly be ascribed to pessimism or bile if it were presented for its own sake. However, at the heart of Pascal's whole *Apology* is the notion of original sin, of a Fall followed by a whole series of historical events, culminating in a Redemption, and still working themselves out. To the proposition 'Nature is corrupt, proved by nature itself' belongs the corollary 'There is a Redeemer, proved by Scripture' (6). Without this idea of a Redeemer the gap between creator and creature, infinite and finite, remains unbridgeable; without the idea of a Fall, a Redeemer makes no sense. The *felix culpa* of the Scholastics, that happy guilt to which the Incarnation and Redemption were God's reply, is central to Pascal's view of Christianity, but for some reason many critics have fastened instead on another theme, that of the hidden God, as representative of Pascal's *Apology* and of Jansenism (however defined) in general. They are right to select the hidden God as a crucial concept, quite wrong to interpret the phrase in a negative, literal way incompatible with Pascal's argument.

All the facts adduced in the first part of the *Apology* are verifiable by observation of ourselves and the world around us. Embedded in this observation is a hypothesis about human history, namely the Fall, which would explain better than any other available hypotheses man's present unhappiness and his persistent search for happiness. Part of the unhappiness involves a view of the individual's future after death, and of man's incapacity, left to himself, to find any reassurance about the hereafter. Thus in a fundamental sense the first half gives a picture of human wretchedness in the present set against human origins in the remotest past and human destiny in a timeless future. The hypothesis of the *felix culpa*, an original sin affecting all men, linked with an eternal redemption, offered to all men but actually enjoyed by few, is the Christian pattern corresponding to this chronology, and it is with this that Pascal begins the second part of the *Apology*.

No longer mere hypothesis, but historical record preserved in Scripture, the Christian revelation is, for Pascal, unique for its continuity from the first man, and its perpetuity to the end of time. While he had mentioned Christ from time to time in the first part, the proofs of man's wretchedness were largely effected in the context of a remote, omnipotent creator inaccessible to reason, except as an incomprehensible being to be accepted like mathematical infinity. With the unfolding of the faith, this picture, which might reasonably be called that of the hidden God, changes completely so that all the rest of the *Apology* is devoted to a demonstration that Christ fills the whole of human history. In the Old Testament he does so through the Messianic prophecies, in the New Testament by his life and death, his teaching and his example, and thereafter by the Church, his body remaining on earth. Just as the whole first part depends on the premiss of man's wretchedness, so all the second part depends on the authenticity of Scripture as a true and historical record, and much else besides. The fact that Pascal's exegesis has not stood the test of time would not necessarily invalidate his argument if some improved modern form of exegesis could supply much the same guarantee of Scriptural authenticity, but it is essential to his argument that the Christian revelation should be demonstrable by Scripture and not be just an edifying mythology or mystery religion.

The consequence of this insistence on Scripture is twofold: it leads to a very precise view of human history and to a very precise view of Christ's place therein. In modern terms, Pascal, like most of his contemporaries, was a fundamentalist. He believed that there was a first man, Adam, created in a state of grace, from which at an identifiable moment in world history he fell through sin; that the span of generations from Adam to Moses as recorded in the Bible corresponded to actual generations, so that Moses set down the history of mankind as it had come down to him in continuous oral transmission from his forebears; that the prophets, and especially the Messianic prophets, were speaking of a historically verifiable period in their future, and that the coming of Christ exactly fulfilled those prophecies. Otherwise, in Pascal's view, the Old Testament is a fable, and the New Testament fulfils nothing. Together with the literal interpretation thus understood, Pascal attached great, perhaps greater, importance to typology, what he called *figures*, and in fact most of the hidden God theme derives from this emphasis on typology.

In the present confused and contradictory state of Biblical scholarship, it would be an unprofitable exercise to attempt a reconstruction of Pascal's argument in the light of modern knowledge. It is none the less only right to insist that his conversion in no way modified his scientific approach, his respect for facts and his intellectual openness. He learned some, not very much, Hebrew so that he could take account of Rabbinical sources of Old Testament scholarship; he would beyond doubt have eagerly absorbed all the archaeological, linguistic, literary and other skills useful and necessary for exegesis today; and he would not have advanced any argument without the fullest investigation of the evidence. It is equally certain that he would have repudiated as distasteful blasphemy any book bearing the title 'The Myth of God Incarnate'. But it is possible to go further and propose what Pascal would have regarded as the irreducible minimum of Christian doctrine.

Man, he believed, was different in kind, not just in degree, from the animals, as he possessed an immortal soul and the power of reason. There must therefore have been a moment in time when the first creature, or creatures, so endowed appeared. Up to that moment no moral choice had been made on earth, but with the advent of morality, however interpreted, man became the first creature to rebel against his creator and his environment. This rebellion may be seen as a sense of estrangement in human life, and for Pascal was inseparable from its effects on the eternal life for which man alone of all creatures had been created. Realisation of these primitive truths about mankind formed part of the Jewish tradition and religion, and their role as God's chosen people was essential in Pascal's scheme because with the tradition of the Fall they also presented faith in a future Messiah, who would redeem them from that Fall. Whatever part of the truth other races and religions may have had or still possess, Pascal could never have compromised on the unique historic incarnation recorded in the Gospels. That incarnation, in his view, was truly God becoming man. With Christ's death and resurrection, the promise of eternal life was restored, and with it the possibility of overcoming wretchedness in man's life on earth. It will be seen that the essential propositions – the Fall, Incarnation and Redemption – are still matters of pure faith, not of rational demonstration, while all the rationally disputable facts – origin of the species, place of the Jewish people, historicity of the two Testaments – are open to considerable, though not indefinite, modification.

The related themes of the hidden God and typology carry the argument one stage further, and reintroduce the theory of orders in a rather different context from that so far seen. One of the objections made by unbelievers is that if the revelation of God in the prophets, and fulfilment in the Gospels, is so certain, how do Christians account for the failure of almost all Jews and a large number of Gentiles to see it? An early answer to this objection comes in the section 'Foundations' and concludes with the key quotation from Isaiah XLV, 15: 'That God wished to hide himself. If there were only one religion God would be clearly manifest. If there were no martyrs except in our religion God would likewise be manifest. God being thus hidden, any religion which does not say that God is hidden is not true, and any religion which does not explain why does not instruct. Ours does all this. "Verily thou art a God that hidest thyself" ' (24). The very long fragment (427), probably contemporaneous with the Wager, says exactly the same in greater detail:

If this religion boasted that it had a clear sight of God and plain and manifest evidence of his existence, it would be an effective objection to say that there is nothing to be seen in the world which proves him so obviously. But since on the contrary it says that men are in darkness and remote from God, that he has hidden himself from their understanding, that this is the very name which he gives himself in Scripture: *Deus absconditus* [the hidden God] ... the obscurity in which they find themselves ... far from proving the Church's teaching false, confirms it.

One of the ways in which God thus hides himself is in the *figures* of the Bible, as 'when David foretold that the Messiah would deliver his people from their enemies, we may believe that, according to the flesh, he meant the Egyptians' (269). In fact, Pascal maintains, the enemies in question are the people's iniquities. In a whole series of fragments, Pascal lists these 'carnal errors', which misled the 'carnal Jews' just as similar errors mislead 'gross Christians' – the 'Jews of the new law' – 'who believe that the Messiah has dispensed them from loving God'.(286) The opposite of 'carnal' or 'concupiscence' is 'charity', and Pascal clearly states the rule: 'Everything which does not lead to charity is figurative. The sole object of Scripture is charity' (270). The reference to gross Christians is obviously aimed at the Jesuits and their supporters, who, according to the Tenth *PL*, claimed exactly that the Gospel dispenses men from 'the tiresome necessity of loving God', but the reference to charity is crucial.

In section 23, 'Proofs of Jesus Christ', comes the fullest and clearest exposition of the theory of orders in its final, apologetic, form, and at the same time a complete answer to the problem of the hidden God. One of the difficulties with Pascal is to establish his terminology. In a fragment from 'Foundations' he had written: 'God wishes to move the will rather than the mind' (234), and this is paralleled in the later formulation:

The heart has its order, the mind has its own, which uses principles and demonstrations ... Jesus Christ and St Paul possess the order of charity, not of the mind, for they wished to humble, not to teach ... This order consists mainly in digressions upon each point which relates to the end, so that this shall be kept always in sight. (298)

Heart and will can be moved by higher or by lower impulses, downwards by concupiscence to become carnal and gross, upwards by charity to become spiritual; but it is this movement, and not intellectual assent, with which religion and the spiritual life are concerned. Confusion of the three orders, or failure to use them properly, results in just that blindness of which the hidden God is the expression.

One fragment in particular sums up in almost lyrical stanzas many of the arguments of the *Apology*:

The infinite distance between body and mind symbolises the infinitely more infinite distance between mind and charity, for charity is supernatural . . . The greatness of wisdom, which is nothing if it does not come from God, is not visible to carnal or intellectual people. They are three orders differing in kind . . . All bodies, the firmament, the stars, the earth and its kingdoms are not worth the least of minds, for it knows them all and itself too, while bodies know nothing. All bodies together and all minds together and all their products are not worth the least impulse of charity. This is of an infinitely superior order. (308)

The theory of orders, the dignity of thought, the insufficiency of man's dual nature, the hidden God: all are there.

Now at last it appears that man is capable of better things. The penultimate section, 'Christian Morality', makes good the double claim 'Happiness of man with God – that there is a Redeemer.' In typical antitheses, Pascal writes: 'Wretchedness induces despair, Pride induces presumption. The Incarnation shows man the greatness of his wretchedness through the greatness of the remedy required' (352), and again: 'There is no doctrine better suited to man than that which teaches him his dual capacity for receiving and losing grace, on account of the dual danger to which he is exposed of despair and pride' (354). The result is as promised: 'No one is as happy as a true Christian, or so reasonable, virtuous and lovable' (357), which recalls the closing sentences of the Wager, on the consequences for this life of opting for Christianity. Similarly balance is restored when the context is complete: 'How little pride the Christian feels in believing himself united to God! How little he grovels when he likens himself to the earthworm! A fine way to meet life and death, good and evil!' (358). The lonely terror in the cosmos, the solitary death or the domineering ego all alike find their cure in the Christian revelation. A comparison of the members with the body brings this out:

The separated member . . . believes itself to be whole . . . believes itself to be dependent only on itself and tries to make itself its own centre and body . . . *He that is joined to the Lord is one spirit*

(I Corinthians VI, 17), we love ourselves because we are members of Christ. We love Christ because he is the body of which we are members. All are one. (372)

Thus Pascal justifies the categorical statements at the beginning of the second part of the *Apology*: 'We know God only through Jesus Christ. Without this mediator all communication with God is broken off' (189), and 'It is not only impossible but useless to know God without Christ' (191). Another fragment adds:

we only know ourselves through Jesus Christ; we only know life and death through Jesus Christ. Apart from Jesus Christ we cannot know the meaning of our life and our death, of God or of ourselves. Thus without Scripture, whose only object is Christ, we know nothing, and can see nothing but obscurity and confusion in the nature of God and in nature itself. (417)

Alternatively, as a phrase in a longer fragment puts it, 'Jesus Christ is the object of all things, the centre towards which all things tend. Whoever knows him knows the reason for everything' (446). The same fragment makes the point that deism and atheism are equally abhorrent to Christianity, and goes on to claim: 'But for Christ the world would not go on existing, for it would either have to be destroyed or be a kind of hell.' Far from being a terrible hidden God, the God revealed in Christ is a God of love and consolation.

Here, finally, one can see that the order of charity really does mean for Pascal the order of divine love, without which all remains chaotic and hostile to man. The implications of such a view of Christ are almost endless. The fundamental consequence of accepting it is that man can find a new harmony within himself, body and mind working together instead of at odds, in obedience to the heart, ruled by love and charity. Man's innate selfishness gives way to a new relationship to all other men, members like him of the Church, the body of Christ, and like him working for the good of the whole and not the isolated member. Acknowledgement of wretchedness brings humility, instead of despair, acknowledgement of greatness brings faith and hope, instead of pride. The cosmos no longer oppresses man, who transcends it just as Christ had conquered death. Above all

man is freed from the prison of his own inadequacy, so that
instead of trying to make a God through reason in his own image
(deism), instead of trying to gratify his own material desires (car-
nality and concupiscence), he submits at last to the love of God,
looking upwards instead of inwards. Perfect love casts out fear,
and the God whose mercy to us was shown in the Incarnation
and Redemption of Christ has already given us the love which we
have only to accept to reciprocate. 'Since we are all corrupt and
incapable of loving God, God made himself man in order to
unite himself with us' (381).

The happiness thus attained is not merely a state of mind but
also a way of life. 'Two laws are enough to rule the whole Christian republic better than all political laws' (376), but the
second follows the first and is inseparable from it. Unselfish,
disinterested love of our fellows is the basis and condition of
Christian morality. Good works are essential, not because they
earn us salvation or even happiness, but because we cannot love
God and keep his commandments without them. What makes
them good, however, is not the pleasure of the beneficiary or
respect gained for the benefactor, but solely the love of God
prompting them.

There remains the question of election to and membership of
the Church, where, if anywhere, Pascal's Jansenism would appear.
As a matter of historical fact, few men in any generation, Jews or
Christians, seem to have kept the faith in the way required by
Scripture, but the survival of that faith proves that there were
always enough men so to do. It is obvious that Pascal would not
have addressed his *Apology* to the worldly unbeliever whose fail-
ings he so frequently lists if he had believed that anyone was
disqualified at any moment in his life from sharing in the fruits
of Christ's Redemption. It is plain, too, that those Christians
whom he called 'carnal' were false, though in an external sense
they belonged to the Church. When they say 'Jesus Christ came
to dispense us from loving God, and to give us sacraments which
are fully efficacious without our help' (287) he categorically
denies that they are Christians and, to that extent, numbered
among the elect, though they too are eligible for conversion. In
several places Pascal distinguishes types of error, but schism, to

his mind, is more serious than disputes within the Church, because it makes disobedience a positive principle, rather than a disagreement, which could be healed. A crucial fragment states his view:

There would be too much darkness if there were no visible signs of the truth. One admirable sign of it is that it has always resided in a visible truth and congregation. There would be too much light if there were only one opinion in the Church. That which has always existed is the true one, for the true one has always been there, but no false one has always been there. (758)

Once more perpetuity is the criterion of truth, truth the criterion of the Church.

Perhaps the last word on this difficult subject of the hidden God is to be found in the last fragment of the section on 'Miracles', included in the *Pensées* though not intended for the *Apology*:

When you say that Christ did not die for all men, you are abusing a weakness of men, who at once apply this exception to themselves, and this encourages despair, instead of turning them away from it to encourage hope. For in this way one accustoms oneself to inward virtues by outward habits. (912)

If the blatant enemies of truth are thereby cutting themselves off from God and happiness, Pascal could not make it clearer that for all men of good will Christ's offer of redemption stands, and no one can say of anyone else that it has failed, only that it has been rejected.

7 Personal spirituality

All the texts so far discussed from the period after Pascal's conversion were devised with a particular audience and adversary in view. *The Conversation with M. de Saci*, the *PLs* and the *Pensées* in their polemical or apologetic ways show clearly what Pascal thought about his faith in what might be called the public sector. In response to specific questions or challenges, we all formulate our faith rather differently from what was the case when it remained purely private. Furthermore, there is a tendency to put words into the mouth of an interlocutor which may be a false projection of our own case rather than a true expression of his. This has always been a major argument of Pascal's critics, who maintain that the wretchedness attributed to the interlocutor is a pure figment of Pascal's imagination. Whatever the force of such an argument, and it cannot be dismissed out of hand, there is undoubtedly a case for attempting to define Pascal's personal, private spirituality divorced from a polemical context. This is all the more important in that the turning-point of his life, his conversion, was an intensely private experience, only communicable in part, and in fact not communicated at all until the chance discovery of the record after his death. There survive other private papers to give an insight into his spiritual life and set his published religious writings in a somewhat fuller perspective.

It cannot be said too often that Pascal was not an advocate speaking to a brief in which he was only partly involved; he was committed totally to the faith he expounds and defends. One does not need to be a convert in order to undertake the task of converting others, but no one who has undergone a conversion experience can fail to use it as a yardstick in approaching that task. It is therefore right and necessary to begin with Pascal's own conversion.

Unlike Pascal's first conversion at Rouen, this second and decisive experience did not directly involve anyone else, though his sister Jacqueline had been very much in his mind, and the

Port-Royal authorities must have had some influence in representing his Christian duty to her and them. Pascal was very much alone on the night of 23 November 1654, and showed no one the record (generally known as the *Memorial*) which he made of his experience. It was, he believed, a direct revelation and call made to him and achieved what no amount of discussion, thought or even prayer had done up till then. The thirty or so lines contain eight quotations from Scripture, some written in Latin, some in French, with three of the four New Testament ones significantly from St John's Gospel, on which he had probably been meditating. The remaining brief entries include several repetitions, especially of the name of Jesus, and are descriptive of a state of mind, or more exactly of heart, at last granted relief from unbearable tension and alienation. The whole experience lasted some two hours, from 10.30 p.m., and should be seen as a sequence of meditations, free but intense, centred on Christ. The alienation is from Christ in person ('I have cut myself off from him') and not from a God vaguely conceived.

From the cryptic opening entry, 'Fire', written as a heading, the experience is usually called 'the night of fire'. While no possibility can be excluded, it seems unlikely that Pascal saw anything (tongues of flame, for example), but rather felt an inner warmth and radiance replace the cold of separation. Such an interpretation is supported by the line coming roughly half-way through: 'joy, joy, joy, tears of joy!' In between comes a series of contrasts: 'God of Abraham, God of Isaac, God of Jacob, not of philosophers and scholars', a clear rejection of intellectual pretensions and acceptance of Biblical tradition. 'The world forgotten, and everything except God', which is self-explanatory, is followed by the cryptic 'Greatness of the human soul'. 'I have cut myself off from him' is followed by the plea 'Let me not be cut off from him for ever!', and a little later the same 'I have cut myself off from him' is expanded with 'shunned him, denied him, crucified him', followed by 'Let me never be cut off from him.' After the earlier 'the world forgotten . . .' he had written 'He can only be found by the ways taught in the Gospels', but now, at the end of the meditation, he puts 'kept' in place of 'found', followed by 'sweet and total renunciation'. Two lines

possibly added some years later none the less belong to the experience: 'Total submission to Jesus Christ and my direc-
tor/Everlasting joy in return for one day's effort on earth', which
seems to prefigure the very terms of the argument of the Wager.

When, at the end of the Wager, Pascal tells his interlocutor
that the preceding attempts at persuasion came from a man who
had gone down on his knees before and after, it must be assumed
that the prayer had been along the lines of his own conversion
experience. Intellectual pride ('God ... not of philosophers and
scholars') and the lure of worldly values (set against 'the ways
taught in the Gospels') had caused the alienation, so intellect
must abate its claims and the world must be forgotten. At the
centre of Pascal's experience, and all his subsequent faith, stands
the Cross: a feeble creature may rebel in order to assert himself
against an omnipotent and remote creator, but the man on the
Cross is a man like us. To 'shun, deny, crucify' Christ is
selfishness, not bold rebellion; it is to turn one's back on the only
man fully to share, in order fully to redeem, human wretchedness. Equally, 'total submission to Jesus Christ and my director'
means renouncing the self in all its manifestations. Pascal's 'certainty', like the 'tears of joy', came from the heart, and thenceforth all his appeals to intellect were designed to remove obstacles
so that the heart, not the mind, was free to accept the truth.

Another text of great force and beauty is the *Mystery of Jesus*
(919), a meditation in poetic prose on the Passion, probably composed not long after the *Memorial*, but only published in 1844.
Here in sustained form is an expression of the same identification
with Christ seen in the *Memorial*. The theme is Jesus' total aban-
donment in the garden of Gethsemane: his three dearest friends
fail him at this moment of agony by falling asleep.

Jesus seeks companionship and solace from men. It seems to me
that this is unique in his whole life, but he finds none, for his disciples
are asleep. Jesus will be in agony until the end of the world. There
must be no sleeping during that time.

The implication of the last two phrases is to put the Gospel story
into the present for every one of us, to involve each Christian as
the disciples were involved, but with the difference that we

cannot plead ignorance of the consequences if we fall asleep. In this context, Pascal's indignation against those who, like Montaigne, prefer the soft pillow of ignorance and inertia can be better understood.

Pascal continues the meditation on the agony in the garden, and then puts a series of remarks into Jesus' mouth echoing more fully the general lines of the *Memorial*. In some sense, it might be argued that this is Pascal talking to himself, but while there is no reason to suppose that his experience of Christ's presence included hearing voices, such verbalisation undoubtedly conveyed Pascal's response to feelings (he would say 'grace') originating from outside himself. The first of these exclamations is the best known: 'Take comfort; you would not seek me if you had not found me.' A little later we read: 'My concern is for your conversion; do not be afraid and pray with confidence as though for me' and 'Endure the chains and bondage of the body. For the present I am delivering you only from spiritual bondage.' The last words of this meditation show once more Pascal's extraordinary ability to relate the most profound spiritual truths to daily reality: 'Do small things as if they were great, because of the majesty of Christ, who does them in us and lives our life, and great things as if they were small and easy, because of his almighty power.'

A further set of documents of a private nature, though destined this time to be read by others, is the incomplete series of Pascal's letters addressed to Charlotte de Roannez, but intended also for the eyes of her brother, the duke. Nine of them survive, in extracts, written between September and December 1656. Coming so soon after Pascal's conversion and the miracle of the Holy Thorn, the letters are particularly interesting as revealing something of Pascal's relationship with two intimate friends and for their bearing on Charlotte's vocation to become a nun, which came to nothing and in which the duke never really believed.

The early letters treat the theme of detachment, from the world in a bad sense but also from the legitimate ties which prevent complete submission to God's will. In the *Pensées* Pascal writes more than once of the dangers of forming attachments to others as mortal as ourselves, such as those of family, and even of the obligation he felt to prevent others forming such attachments towards him. This is quite different from the detachment taught by the Stoics, whose end was self-mastery and freedom from passions, and who in practice often seemed callous. Perhaps Pascal's painful experience with his sister had brought this truth home to him, but he believes that one cannot do God's will if bound by human ties. In the matter of religious vocation such ties must be a major factor.

The fourth letter brings in the theme of the hidden God, in connection with the recent official recognition as miraculous of cures effected by the Holy Thorn. Pascal traces the successive stages of God's concealment, first under the veil of nature, then, at the Incarnation, under the veil of humanity and finally under the veil of the Eucharist. The veils of nature and of humanity were pierced by some pagans and by Christian heretics who otherwise missed the truth, but to Catholics alone is vouchsafed the revelation of Christ in the sacrament. He pursues the theme that only the eye of faith penetrates to the hidden truth: 'All things cover some mystery; all things are veils covering God.' But the end of the letter invites Charlotte to praise God, who has hidden himself in everything from others but revealed himself in so many ways for 'us', the true believers. As in his less private works, Pascal repeats the theme that the banquet was prepared for a far greater number than accepted the invitation.

The sixth letter carries the idea of the Church a stage further. Here Pascal categorically affirms that all virtues, martyrdoms and good works are useless outside the Church 'and communion with the head of the Church who is the Pope. I will never separate myself from this communion, at least I pray God to give me that grace; otherwise I should be lost for ever.' Such sentiments do not deter him from recognising that some within the Church, and theoretically even the Pope, may fall into error, but what he himself calls his profession of faith cannot be set aside in interpreting the *Pensées*. The emphasis is on communion, on unity, not on blind obedience, and the simile of the head and the members is very much to the fore. We know the anguish he, and his friends, underwent when blind obedience was demanded of them in signing a declaration they believed to be factually wrong, but if the Church (however defined) is the body of Christ, Pascal had no choice but to remain within it. In the last analysis blind obedience was his only way.

The seventh letter is an excellent illustration of Pascal's habits of mind and style, and shows beyond doubt that in private as in public these were identical. A whole set of antitheses and triple patterns exactly recalls similar patterns in his published work. The basic argument is that pains and pleasures are equally necessary for salvation; the pain of the Cross and the pleasure of finding Christ. The way, he says, is neither physical austerity nor mental disturbance, but proper disposition of the heart. The whole letter is a lyrical celebration of the joys of faith, and attributes all sadness not to true piety but to the remaining vestiges of impiety. Just as the triple exclamation of joy came at the heart of the *Memorial*, and of the experience it records, so here, in a private letter to intimate friends, the accent is all on joy. This needs saying, because for many people Jansenism is synonymous with gloom, and Pascal is often made out to be some kind of joyless puritan. In fact it is faith in the pure joy to come, already prefigured in his conversion, that provides the motive force for his religion.

The eighth letter introduces an idea frequently met in the *Pensées*: 'The present is the only time which really belongs to us.' He goes on to say that if we only obey the Gospel precept to take no heed for the morrow, it will bring us to salvation and to peace of mind. The last letter reminds his correspondents that we are bidden to bear Christ's yoke, not our own, and that for Christ, but not for us, it is light and gentle.

What emerges from these private and personal texts is not at all unexpected, but it is good to have expectations confirmed by evidence. Pascal's conversion brought him into what he regarded as a personal relationship with Christ, which thenceforth formed the core of his whole life. The experience brought him lasting joy, which he tries to communicate to others; it brought him a new insight into the Gospels, which showed him all he needed to know for the daily conduct of his life; and also, in the *Mystery of Jesus*, it actualised past events, so that through the Gospels he could share the life of Christ on earth. No less important, his conversion and subsequent life brought him into a new relationship with the Church, and his director, so that neither pride nor loneliness separated him from the body of Christ, the body of the faithful.

If the religion thus apprehended was firmly based in the heart, it demanded full and constant contribution from body (in external habits) and mind (in studying Scripture and the Church's doctrine). It is probably true to say that Pascal's faith had become the childlike faith of the simple, so often praised in the *Pensées*, but it is certainly untrue that his intellectual integrity was compromised or forgotten. It is a common experience to find that intellectual and emotional maturity bring simplification of problems, even of style. Once Pascal clearly saw the patterns and priorities, everything fell into place in an integrated whole view of the world, God and man.

Conclusion

It has been a major contention of this study that Pascal's life is inseparable from his work, in particular the *Pensées*, and that habits of mind originally acquired in a scientific context persisted after his conversion, when he turned his attention to religion. In itself such a thesis would, of course, be of little use in accounting for the continuing popularity of Pascal, not only in his own country and his own language but throughout the Western world, and, indeed, as far afield as Japan, where distinguished work on Pascal is being done. Some people no doubt read Pascal out of historical interest, in the same way that they might read Descartes or Locke, some for literary reasons, because even in translation his style is arresting: but no serious approach to Pascal today can ignore the fact that for countless readers throughout the world Pascal apparently fills a need. The adding-machine, the experiments of the vacuum, the wit of the *PLs* all arouse interest, but the book that annually sells its thousands of copies is the *Pensées*. After three hundred years something more than a prima facie case has evidently been made out: Pascal and the *Pensées* are incontrovertibly important today, and show no sign of becoming less so. At the end of such a brief study as this no definitive conclusion can be offered, but to offer none would be indefensible.

When Pascal said of Montaigne that what we find in him is really in ourselves, he provided the critic, as has already been mentioned, with a convenient starting-point. To the extent that each reader finds something of himself in Pascal, the *Pensées* can claim universal appeal. Behind that convenient formula, however, must lie some deeper truth about the readers; Pascal would say about man. At one level, this truth concerns perception and communication. As a mathematician of genius, Pascal had the gift of abstract thought enjoyed by very few, and he showed equal ability in presenting cogent rational arguments. To that extent his early training fitted him for the apologetic task he later set himself. It is clear in the *Pensées* that Pascal knows what he is talking about, and that he is not just playing with words, even when, as in the Wager argument, non-mathematical readers miss the finer points. Where Pascal scores over equally gifted mathematicians and logicians, even over Descartes, is in his power to represent the most abstract truths in concrete form, to appeal to the imagination as well as to pure reason and to carry the reader with him.

Pascal has the gift of every successful teacher: he makes the reader see for himself what has always been dimly present before his eyes, and articulates the new vision in memorable verbal form. This is what Descartes so splendidly achieved in the earlier parts of his *Discourse on Method*, introducing philosophy to the layman, but he followed it up in the later parts with examples of the rigorously mathematical and logical method of the title. All great writers make us see for ourselves so that the vision in some sense becomes truly our own. Pascal is an incomparably better writer than Descartes, but in the history of philosophy he is allotted very much less space. He did not offer a system, nor even a method in the Cartesian sense, though his subject matter was no less extensive and the claims made for his method (if the theory of orders can be so described) are no less far-reaching. He was a powerful and original thinker, but he would not claim, in Descartes' sense, to be a philosopher: the first line of the *Memorial* once and for all rejected the God 'of philosophers and scholars'.

In terms, then, of the deeper truths about ourselves, is it possible further to define Pascal's significance? He as usual gives the best answer: 'Let no one say that I have said nothing new; the arrangement of the material is new. In playing tennis both players use the same ball, but one plays it better' (696). One is tempted to leave that memorable image to work its magic. In that sentence Pascal both eliminates the distance between himself and the reader, who grasps the point immediately, and, perhaps unconsciously, asserts his superiority in the last word. The assumption must be, as with any good teacher, that once the reader has absorbed the lesson the superiority will disappear, or at least cease to matter. The purpose of the *Apology* is manifestly to achieve such equality, but until it is complete the steps towards it are marked by points of identity established between Pascal and the reader. Of these the fundamental one seems to be search into questions regarding man's true nature and destiny, his relationship to other men, to the world around him and to a God, if God exists. Pascal's frequent attacks against those who do not search are more important than they may appear. Most philosophers, Descartes for example, claim emphatically to have found, and expect the reader either to accept the truth proclaimed or to follow the steps prescribed, which will infallibly lead them to it. There will always be such dogmatists, and they will always provoke reaction from sceptics, but it is not among either that most of Pascal's readers will be found. The phrase already quoted from the *Mystery of Jesus* establishes community of purpose, even if it leaves open equality of status: 'Take comfort; you would not seek me if you had not found me.' Compare this with the full title of Descartes' definitive work: 'Meditations concerning the first [basic] philosophy in which the existence of God and the real distinction between the body and soul are demonstrated.' So confident an assertion of the power of reason has not stood the test of time, or even of contemporary critics, but men go on searching.

Pascal addresses himself to those who are willing to seek, who believe neither that they have already found adequate answers to the fundamental questions of life, however formulated, nor that seeking such answers is a waste of time. Many of those who read Pascal are unable, or unwilling, to accept the demands of such commitment to the Christian faith as he describes, but even to those who remain agnostic he offers something of solid worth which should not be seen as second best, and may perhaps be defined as integrity, or wholeness. Intellectual truth is all very well, but it does not feed the spirit or the emotions. 'The heart has its reasons of which reason knows nothing.'

Pascal's analysis of the human condition started from the élite society in which he lived. When he described the frantic need to be busy, the hollowness of social conventions, the arbitrariness and plain injustice of the law, the ever wider spaces, the ever tinier entities revealed by science, the apparent pointlessness of so many lives, the real loneliness of so many more, he was painting substantially the same picture as many other seventeenth-century observers from La Rochefoucauld to La Bruyère. Universal education and wider opportunities for leisure have helped to make such an analysis largely applicable to ordinary modern Western society. On the psychological level, seventeenth-century critics of society attributed its defects to self-interest. On the theological level, self-interest was identified by Augustinians as a perverse alternative to the love of God and neighbour.

In strictly human terms Pascal's Augustinian theology is undeniably pessimistic; he sees the worst in man because he believes in man's fundamental corruption. That is why he rejected all purely human solutions to social or psychological problems, believing that human planning or organisation, however well meant, would always founder eventually on the reef of self-interest. That is why in particular he rejected the boundless optimism that rationalists like Descartes had in the unaided power of human reason to improve man's lot. Other theologians, notably Jesuits, took a much more favourable view of man without necessarily being rationalists, but such teaching had had moral effects so reprehensible as to provoke Augustinian reaction in the first place, and then such a polarisation of attitudes that the always moderate Thomists tended to be eclipsed.

Theology, of course, does not stop at human terms, and it is only when Pascal's view of corrupt human nature is complemented by the inseparable concept of redeemed human nature that the positive element appears. Pascal, like all his friends, was totally committed to the idea that loving God meant loving one's neighbour, even one's enemies. Collective acts of philanthropy, practical use of talents for the good of others (the bonesetters who treated his father, Pascal's bus service), private acts of charity (Pascal's hospitality to an indigent family) may be good in themselves, but for Pascal are part of one's inescapable Christian duty. He believed that unselfishness and devotion to others was an integral part of Christianity, exemplified and revealed by Christ on the Cross. The human solidarity implied in such a belief arises from Christianity, but must, if authentic, be unconditionally extended to all, Christian and non-Christian alike. Such belief can hardly be called pessimistic.

There must be many readers who recognise in Pascal someone who faced up to the most familiar and least palatable truths of human existence in himself. Arguments are less convincing than instinct, and Pascal's finest passages undoubtedly appeal to the emotions. Men faced with death or bereavement, despair or isolation are not consoled by reason, though they must not be made to feel that reason is of no account. In such crises the deepest level of personality is touched and threatened, and however much we may turn to others for reassurance, if it is to be found, we cannot find it by proxy. Pascal more than most writers seems able to make contact at just that deeply personal level. He too has struggled with his own loneliness and selfishness, with fear of the unknown hereafter, and in speaking from his own experience he affirms a human solidarity in which all may share.

Pascal's presentation of Christianity is not the only valid one, perhaps not even the best, but it is unquestionably authentic and based on his personal experience. His conversion enabled him to write the *Pensées*, and he believed that on that November night he had had a direct experience of God's love revealed in the person of Christ. From then on 'Jesus Christ is the centre towards which all things tend.' What Pascal tried to convey in the *Pensées* was the power and warmth of the divine love he felt, so that others might share it. He knew that many, like the disciples, would go on sleeping, and many, like the Jews, would reject the truth offered to them, but he hoped that some, like him, would search for the truth, even with groans. The one thing no one can mistake is that he has made his unalterable choice, paid his price, won his reward.

Select bibliography

TEXTS

Because of the multiplicity of editions of the *Pensées*, each with different numbering, it is best to stick to the same one, that of L. Lafuma, based on the First Copy, which has been quoted throughout this study:

Pascal, *Pensées*, Livre de Vie, éds du Seuil, 1962.

Pascal, *Oeuvres complètes*, Intégrale, éds du Seuil, 1963 (contains an identical version of the *Pensées*, together with all his other works). Also highly recommended is an edition based for the first time on the Second Copy, and including a concordance with the Lafuma edition:

Pascal, *Pensées*, ed. Philippe Sellier, Mercure de France, 1976.

TRANSLATIONS

Pascal, *Pensées*, trans. A. J. Krailsheimer, Penguin, 1966.

Pascal, *Provincial Letters*, trans. A. J. Krailsheimer, Penguin, 1967.

CRITICAL AND BACKGROUND WORKS

There is a vast critical literature on Pascal, some of which is quite unhelpful. The following brief list gives the best recent books available in English and some very important French ones not translated:

A. Adam, *Histoire de la littérature française au XVIIe siècle*, vol. II, Domat, 1951. (A full picture of the literary, philosophical and social background of the age.)

A. Adam, *Grandeur and Illusion*, Weidenfeld, 1972. (A much abbreviated English version of the above.)

J. H. Broome, *Pascal*, E. Arnold, 1965. (A solid, clear general book.)

P. Humbert, *L'Oeuvre scientifique de Pascal*, Michel, 1947. (Shows importance of Pascal's scientific work in historical context.)

J. Mesnard, *Pascal, L'Homme et l'oeuvre*, Boivin, 1951. English translation *Pascal, His Life and Works*, 1952. (The best general book.)

J. Mesnard, *Les Pensées de Pascal*, SEDES, 1976. (An admirable analysis of text and background.)

J. Miel, *Pascal and Theology*, Johns Hopkins, 1969. (Useful on specific technical issues.)

P. Topliss, *The Rhetoric of Pascal*, Leicester University Press, 1966. (On style and power of persuasion.)

Index

References in **bold** indicate fuller treatment

Past Masters

AQUINAS Anthony Kenny

Anthony Kenny writes about Thomas Aquinas as a philosopher, for readers who may not share Aquinas's theological interests and beliefs. He begins with an account of Aquinas's life and works, and assesses his importance for contemporary philosophy. The book is completed by more detailed examinations of Aquinas's metaphysical system and his philosophy of mind.

DANTE George Holmes

George Homes expresses Dante's powerful originality by identifying the unexpected connections the poet made between received ideas and his own experience. He presents Dante's biography both as an expression of the intellectual dilemma of early Renaissance Florence and as an explanation of the poetic, philosophical and religious themes developed in his works. He ends with a discussion of the *Divine Comedy*, Dante's poetic panorama of hell, purgatory and heaven.

HUME A. J. Ayer

A. J. Ayer begins his study of Hume's philosophy with a general account of Hume's life and works, and then discusses his philosophical aims and methods, his theories of perception and self-identity, his analysis of causation, and his treatment of morals, politics and religion. He argues that Hume's discovery of the basis of causality and his demolition of natural theology were his greatest philosophical achievements.

Past Masters

JESUS Humphrey Carpenter

Humphrey Carpenter writes about Jesus from the standpoint of a historian coming fresh to the subject without religious preconceptions. He examines the reliability of the Gospels, the originality of Jesus's teaching, and Jesus's view of himself. His highly readable book achieves a remarkable degree of objectivity about a subject which is deeply embedded in Western culture.

MARX Peter Singer

Peter Singer identifies the central vision that unifies Marx's thought, enabling us to grasp Marx's views as a whole. He views him as a philosopher primarily concerned with human freedom, rather than as an economist or social scientist. He explains alienation, historical materialism, the economic theory of *Capital*, and Marx's idea of communism, in plain English, and concludes with a balanced assessment of Marx's achievement.